How To Be A Self-Published Author

A STEP-BY-STEP GUIDE

ALSO BY PAT GAUDETTE

How to Survive Your Husband's Midlife Crisis:
Strategies and Stories from The Midlife Wives Club,
by Pat Gaudette & Gay Courter

Advice for an Imperfect Single World

Advice for an Imperfect Married World

Midnight Confessions: True Stories of Adultery

Sparky the AIBO: Robot Dogs & Other Robotic Pets

Teen Mom: A Journal

How To Be A Self-Published Author

A STEP-BY-STEP GUIDE

Pat Gaudette

Home & Leisure Publishing, Inc.

Published by
Home & Leisure Publishing, Inc.
P O Box 968
Lecanto, FL 34460-0968
www.halpi.com

First edition: November 2009

EAN-13: 978-0-9825617-0-6
ISBN-10: 0-9825617-0-9

Library of Congress Control Number: 2009909981

This publication is designed to provide information in regard to the subject matter covered. It is sold with the understanding that the publisher and the author are not engaged to render legal, accounting, or other professional services. If legal advice or other expert assistance is required, the services of a competent professional should be sought.

Printed in the United States of America

*Writing is the only profession where no one considers
you ridiculous if you earn no money.*
– Jules Renard (1864-1910)

Contents

Introduction

I changed careers in 1984, leaving the corporate world of pension plans and group insurance to join my former husband's small magazine publishing business. We published a monthly free housing magazine, designed and printed promotional materials for housing communities, and occasionally produced sales videos for housing communities.

Despite our other projects, the core of the business was publishing. We didn't use computers or desktop publishing programs. Pages were made up of pieces of art and pasted type. We relied on typesetting services, color separation companies, and other services to make the magazines press-ready.

Occasionally, when the magazine went to press, we would watch as the first copies were printed. It was exciting to hear the web press start up and watch as the pages raced past on their way to the collator and bindery. That experience continued, even after we added computers and trained our staff to use desktop publishing software.

Offset printing and web presses are still very much a part of the publishing business but there is competition now from digital printing companies – companies who "print on demand" one or more copies, when needed. Digital printing has not just changed the way many publishing houses do business. Digital printing makes it possible for authors to self-publish without investing thousands of dollars in offset printing.

I understand the old way of publishing, when it took several people to make a publication press-ready, and the new way, when one person can do it all. This book explains the new way of publishing a book. ~ Pat Gaudette

Self-Publishing
Is Not Rocket Science

It has never been easier for anyone who has written a book to also have it published. There are many steps involved in publishing a book whether a major publisher is the one in charge or a self-publisher is making the decisions and doing the work, but it's not rocket science.

Today's technology makes it fairly simple for authors who are computer savvy, to also be publishers. The purpose of this book is to provide the steps to self publish a book using online resources and Microsoft Word.

You may not currently have the skills necessary to create a press-ready document, but the more you are willing to learn, the more control you will have over the final published book and the more money you will save.

In this book I provide complete step-by-step details so that you can have a published book for sale on Amazon.com, their affiliated sites, other online booksellers, and in your own online bookstore. If you want more distribution, I also show how to publish your book through Lightning Source. Lastly, I show you how to publish an ebook for Amazon's Kindle and other digital readers.

Occasionally, a self-published book will turn into a best-seller that major publishers can't ignore, but books such as Daniel Suarez' *Daemon* are rare. IT professional Suarez self-published *Daemon*, his first novel, after literary agents showed no interest.

Originally writing under the pseudonym of Leinad Zeraus (his name spelled backwards), Suarez and his wife, also an IT professional, set up their own publishing company and used the print on demand resources of Lightning Source to produce the book. If they had stopped there, *Daemon* might still be an undiscovered treasure.

But the Suarez' promotional efforts among the virtual world of gamers and bloggers – *Daemon* is a thriller *about* gaming in the virtual world – generated tremendous online buzz and excellent book sales.

Major publishers took notice and, in January 2009, *Daemon* was published by Dutton, a member of Penguin Group (USA) Inc. A follow-up novel is in the works, DreamWorks has acquired the film rights, and *Daemon* has been translated into ten foreign languages.

Suarez' success is not typical; all elements meshed together to create a best-selling book. Some self-published books are poorly written but so are some books published by major publishing houses.

Self-publishing is not new. Virginia Woolf, James Joyce, Walt Whitman, William Blake, William Morris, Tom Peters, James Redfield, Oscar Wilde, Phyllis Schlafly, E.E. Cummings, Deepak Chopra, Benjamin Franklin, Zane Grey, Upton Sinclair, Gearge Bernard Shaw, Mark Twain, Thomas Paine, D.H. Lawrence, Carl Sandburg, and Rudyard Kipling all self-published.

Current technology makes it easy to self-publish a book, which means along with some exceptional books rejected by traditional publishing houses, plenty of mediocre and just plain awful books are being published.

But so what? Even major publishing houses occasionally publish clunkers. Readers will be the ultimate judge and jury as they always have been.

Regardless of how a book gets published, getting published may be the easiest step. Because readers will determine whether or not a book is a "success" in terms of sales, smart marketing and publicity are critical.

Most self-published books sell a few hundred copies at best with authors lucky if they can make back their initial investment. Being published, even by a major publishing house, does not guarantee a book will turn into a best-seller or the author will become wealthy. The harsh reality is that it takes major marketing and promotional work to generate book sales and, even then, sales numbers may not be large enough to recoup the expenses of publishing and marketing the book.

I don't want to discourage anyone from self-publishing, but I do want to dispel the thought that a published book means instant wealth and celebrity. Perhaps yours *will* be the book that sells a million copies, but don't bet your savings on it. And don't quit your day job until it happens.

There are three steps to publishing a book: Writing it, publishing it, and marketing it. There are many good books written that focus on each of these steps. This book will focus on publishing a book.

First Things
First

To become a published author, you should have a business plan in place, and a completed manuscript in hand.

You can write anywhere, anytime, but when you decide to become a (self) published author, you will be spending money (absolutely), earning money (hopefully), and dealing with the normal business issues that are a part of being published regardless of how this occurs.

Consult with professionals who can help determine what type of business you should set up as each type has advantages and disadvantages.

If you're a U.S. citizen, you already pay taxes, but, any money you make as a published author is also taxable so you need to keep accurate records of what you earn and what you spend. *Entrepreneur Magazine's Start Your Own Self-Publishing Business: Your Step-by-Step Guide to Success* is a good book for tips about the business side of self-publishing.

Writer's Block

No one can motivate you to finish your book. Either the words are flowing or they're not. You're either passionate about your topic or you're not. With passion, it can be difficult to know when to stop writing. Without passion, it's almost impossible to start.

At one time or another every author runs into that brick wall known as "writer's block." Most published authors don't worry about it, they keep writing until they work through it, or they do something else to clear their mind and refocus.

If you haven't finished writing your book, finish it. If you don't have a completed manuscript, the steps after this one won't be of much use.

If you need help writing your book, step away from this tutorial and talk to someone, search the Web for inspiration, or read some books.

When I first began writing, primarily short stories and poetry, I was most inspired when I was at a typewriter. Any other method, such as sitting with pen to paper, turned off all creative flow. The typewriter has been replaced by a computer and that is still what keeps the creative flow going.

I've tried carrying a tape recorder to catch the brilliant thoughts that always come into my head when I'm away from the computer; turning the recorder on makes every brilliant word disappear. I have tried voice recognition software. The second I turn it on, my mind turns off.

For me, a keyboard inspires and anything else draws a blank. For others, a keyboard is a sure prelude to writer's block.

Recommended Reading:

Beginnings, Middles & Ends, by Nancy Kress;

The First Five Pages: A Writer's Guide to Staying Out of the Rejection Pile, by Noah Lukeman;

Immediate Fiction: A Complete Writing Course, by Jerry Cleaver;

Writing the Memoir: A practical guide to the craft, the personal challenges, and ethical dilemmas of writing your true stories, by Judith Barrington;

Telling Lies for Fun & Profit: A Manual for Fiction Writers, by Lawrence Block;

The Joy of Writing Sex: A Guide for Fiction Writers, by Elizabeth Benedict;

Writing With a Purpose, by James McCrimmon;

How to Write Tales of Horror, Fantasy & Science Fiction, edited by J.N. Williamson.

Critiques:
Don't Take Them Personally

You may not have let anyone read your manuscript while you were writing it, but, once it's done, it's time to get reader feedback.

A word of caution: it isn't always a good idea to ask family or friends to give their "honest" opinions. You don't really want to hear anything but absolute praise for what you've written, do you? Anything other than "I loved it!" or "OMG! It'll be a bestseller!" is going to hurt your feelings.

Some of the most helpful comments you receive may be negative ones, and, if you take them personally instead of in the manner in which they are intended, you'll not only have hurt feelings, you'll miss out on ideas that could make your book better.

Believe me, any negatives will hurt because writing a book is an exceptionally personal process. It doesn't matter how thick-skinned you consider yourself, you *will* take criticism of your writing personally. It's much safer for friends and family to say little or nothing other than to praise your work. Praise, unfortunately, isn't necessarily going to make your book better.

After I completed the original manuscript for *Teen Mom*, I printed copies and asked three trusted friends if they would give me their honest thoughts about the book. All three had negative feelings after reading the book. They felt the story didn't send a strong enough message to teenagers to keep them from making the same mistakes as the girl in the book, that the girl's experience had been "too easy," and that the book needed a "moralistic" ending.

I'd had my own thoughts about the way the book ended but writing an ending other than the one teen mom was living wouldn't have kept the integrity of the story. Because my doubts had been validated by the comments I received, I shelved the book and worked on other projects. Nearly a year later, I found one of the binders and read through it. The story was good and I knew it was worth publishing. I also knew it needed heavy editing.

The final version of *Teen Mom: A Journal* is not the same one my friends critiqued. It is much better because of a series of intense editing sessions which incorporated their suggestions – except for rewriting the ending.

When I was finished with editing, and had completed the layout and design, I sent a copy of the press-ready PDF to another author and waited for her words of praise. Instead, she suggested more changes that I incorporated into the *final* press-ready file.

So, what do you do? Let friends and family critique your precious creation? Publish without anyone else taking a look and offering an opinion? Or hire an editor to red pencil your work? It's a difficult call.

The only way I can find typos, misspellings, and grammatical errors is to put the book aside for several weeks. Looking at a manuscript with "fresh eyes" makes the errors pop. We all make mistakes regardless of how precise we try to be or think we are. That's why I step away and take another look when the words aren't so fresh in my mind.

Finding typos is not editing, and hiring a proofreader is not the same as hiring an editor.

Recommended reading: *The Frugal Editor: Put Your Best Book Forward to Avoid Humiliation and Ensure Success*, by Carolyn Howard-Johnson.

Illustrations, Are They Necessary?

My books generally have few, if any, illustrations because the topics don't require them. When I wrote *Sparky the AIBO*, illustrations and photographs enhanced the text. I also think illustrations are appropriate for some chapters in this book which is why they're included.

Before I had a co-author, a literary agent, and a book contract with The Berkley Publishing Group, a division of Penguin Group (USA), for my book on male midlife crisis, I had already designed the front cover and paid an artist to create a half dozen cartoons to illustrate various chapters of the book.

Once the prepress work began, the publisher's graphic artists had other ideas for the cover, the marketing and editorial teams wanted the book to have a different title than my title *(The Midlife Wives Club),* and I decided the cartoons, while appropriate for the book I originally wrote, didn't work with the new version.

Because I felt strongly that the book would benefit from a few simple illustrations, and I needed an artist to turn my ideas into artwork the publisher would use, I posted a job notice on Guru.com. The stick figure illustrations published in *How to Survive Your Husband's Midlife Crisis: Strategies and Stories from The Midlife Wives Club*, were drawn by Barb Ericksen, a Guru.com freelance artist.

Clipart books were a useful resource during the years I published print magazines. I would scan images, edit them in Adobe Photoshop, and incorporate them into my layouts. I also purchased DVDs with hundreds of thousands of royalty-free images. The clipart books and DVDs have now been replaced by a membership in Clipart.com, an online service. The illustration on the front cover of this book came from Clipart.com.

Some books need photographs – lots of them – to be complete. Authors writing travel guides, or similar books, should carry point & shoot digital cameras at all times. There are many good pocket-size digital cameras on the market that will provide the image quality needed for publishing. As an example, the 10.0-megapixel Canon PowerShot SD1200 IS Digital ELPH, priced under $300, will provide professional quality photos.

You can always supplement your photos with stock photos if you need more. And always remember to give proper copyright credit when using stock photos or illustrations.

Local artists groups or some high schools and colleges may be worth contacting to see if any artists or art students would be interested in providing artwork for your book.

It is appropriate to pay for artwork as well as give illustrator credit in your book. If your illustrator wants ongoing revenue, if they feel use of their artwork gives them ownership rights, or if they're critical of your efforts, rethink using their services.

Some books depend on illustrations to get the story across, for instance, children's books. Now the author and the illustrator are a collaborative effort and each might share equally in cover credits, copyright, and the income from the book.

A word of caution: choose your collaborative partner wisely as this partnership will last the lifetime of the book.

Marketing may get a buyer as far as a bookseller but if the cover doesn't "grab" their interest to make them want to see what's inside, another book on the same topic may get the sale.

Prospective readers will only see a book's full-size cover if it's in a bookstore. Online and in catalogues the cover will be much smaller so the design must be strong enough to be effective in its mini version.

Life Coach Chandra Alexander used Guru.com to find a cover artist when she self-published *TRASHtionalizations (How to Stop Believing Your Own Excuses and Have a Real Relationship)*.

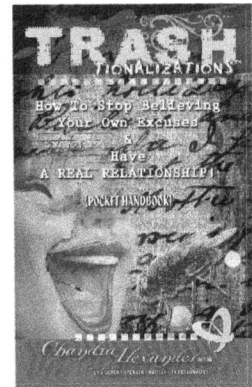

I did the book's pre-press design and layout, incorporating some of the cover art into the page design. The design was also used in marketing materials and on her website.

Gordon Ratcliff wanted a strong font and a torn scroll for the cover of his first novel, *The Judas Fragment*.

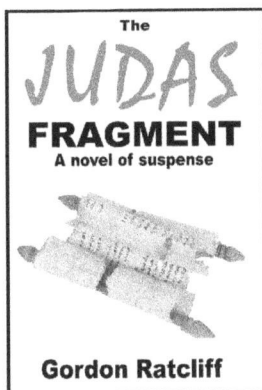

I found a selection of scrolls on Clipart.com, and then provided a variety of typefonts and color schemes for him to choose from.

The cover colors of black and red pop against the white background. Even as a thumbnail, the cover gets the theme across.

Long before I had a co-author, a literary agent, or a publishing contract with Perigee, I had already designed a cover for my book about male midlife crisis.

As enamored as I was with my title (*The Midlife Wives Club*) and cover design, various of the publishing house's staff were not. The editor wasn't negative about the title because she had read the manuscript, but the sales and PR staff were unfamiliar with the subject matter and the title didn't make sense to them. They felt most book retailers and the general book buyer wouldn't understand the title, either.

After much discussion, we all agreed that *How To Survive Your Husband's Midlife Crisis,* with the subtitle *Strategies and Stories from The Midlife Wives Club,* was much better. My cover design didn't work with the new title, and the published cover design was provided by one of the publisher's artists.

I've tried to be more direct with my titles since then because few people will give a second thought to a title that's too vague regardless of how "cute" it might be. I also try to create covers that illustrate the topic and reproduce well as thumbnails.

For my self-published books, I have used a variety of sources for the cover art. The image of "Queenie," on the covers for *Advice for an Imperfect Single World* and *Advice for an Imperfect Married World,* was created by a Guru.com artist.

I used my own photograph on the front cover of *Sparky the AIBO* and photographs provided by other AIBO enthusiasts on the back cover and throughout the text.

A photograph from Clipart.com and heavy editing in Photoshop produced the cover for *Midnight Confessions.*

I paid an artist to create the anime art for *Teen Mom,* then used it to design two different covers, the one to the right for the paperback and a another for the gloss laminate hardcover.

I used art from Clipart.com and CreateSpace's free Cover Creator to design the cover for this book.

Suggested reading: *Book Design and Production: A Guide for Authors and Publishers,* by Pete Masterson.

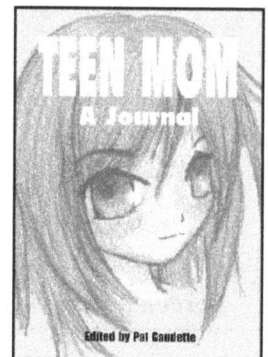

Publishing
Options

There are several ways for an author to become published, some better than others.

Major Publishing Houses

What author wouldn't want the "stamp of approval" that being published by a major publishing house will give them and their book? Let's not forget the potential advance, which could be sizeable. But there are far more good books written than there are major publishing houses willing to publish them.

Publishers such as Berkley, Ballantine, Simon & Schuster, St. Martins Press, HarperCollins, and Doubleday must sell high volumes of books in order to produce good profits for their shareholders. Rather than risk a loss by working with unproven talent, they work with established or celebrity authors.

Sometimes a publisher will regret turning down a new author's book that later becomes a best-seller. Several major publishing houses turned down J.K. Rowling's first book about a young wizard; one smaller publisher didn't.

Subsidy Publishers

Subsidy and print-on-demand is often said in the same breath as though they are the same. They are not. Most subsidy publishers, particularly those who claim extensive distribution through Ingram, use the services of Lightning Source. Lightning Source prints books on offset presses as well as digitally (POD or print-on-demand) for publishing houses of all sizes, including subsidy publishers.

While major publishing houses buy and market a few titles each year, focusing on selling a large volume of books in order to make a profit, subsidy publishers (sometimes referred to as vanity publishers) are more likely to make their profit by selling services to aspiring authors. Some will publish a book at no charge, give the author a small percentage from the sale of each book (royalty), and sell author copies at a fairly high mark-up. Others will charge for editing and pre-press work. Some won't charge for the pre-press production but the author will be required to purchase a large quantity of books at a substantial cost.

It is wise to have an attorney review any contract with a subsidy publisher, prior to signing, so that the legalize doesn't turn a dream into a nightmare. The contract may have fine print that gives the subsidy publisher full rights to the book, payment clauses to hold royalties, and other nasty surprises.

Books won't sell without marketing and some companies will offer a marketing package that may include materials such as stationary, business cards, postcards, and bookmarkers. They may suggest ways to market the book using various media. The author will do the work, and bear all of the expenses. If the author's efforts are successful, the publisher will benefit the most with higher book sales.

Authors with virtually no computer skills may find working with a subsidy publisher the best choice. The publisher will provide editing, layout, design, and everything else needed to actually turn a manuscript into a book.

Not all subsidy publishers are equal or reputable and I strongly recommend reading Mark Levine's *The Fine Print of Self Publishing: The Contracts & Services of 45 Self-Publishing Companies Analyzed Ranked & Exposed* before doing business with any subsidy publisher. Be sure to get the third edition of Levine's book, copyright 2008, or a newer edition if it's available, since subsidy publishing changes constantly. Even though some prices and services have changed since the book was published, the basic information could save a new author literally thousands of dollars!

I visited the Wordclay site after watching a *YouTube* video about their services. The site was very user-friendly with free basic services including an online "publishing wizard." A new author could easily and quickly end up with a book for sale in the Wordclay bookstore.

I was curious how Wordclay fared in Levine's book and found they were listed in the "Publishers to Avoid" section which also included iUniverse and Authorhouse.

Until I read Levine's book, I didn't realize that Wordclay, iUniverse, and Authorhouse all have the same owner.

Wordclay's paid services can be expensive and the author won't own the services they have paid for. For example, an author may pay $999 for a custom cover design but it can only be used through Wordclay; the cover layout files cannot be used to print or publish the book elsewhere.

Finally, one particular sentence in the contract regarding payment of royalties would be enough to make me turn and run from doing business with Wordclay:

> *"We will remit payments to you on a quarterly basis (4 times a year) along with a report of sales in that reported quarter by electronic mail: provided, however, that no payment shall be made to unless and until the amount of the royalties is equal to or exceeds $20,000."*

That's right, if they *owe* royalties of $20,000 or more, the author will be paid. Anything lower and Wordclay keeps the money in *their* bank account. Most authors won't earn anywhere near this much in royalties during their *lifetime*. Fact.

Wordclay is one of many self-publishing/subsidy publishers an author may want to avoid. Mark Levine's book is well worth reading to sift the good from the bad.

CafePress

It is not necessary to be a publisher to print a book through CafePress. Anyone who can produce files to the specifications required, can upload and order copies. Setting up a CafePress store allows sales via links from other websites or when found in searches by visitors to CafePress.

I self-published *Advice for an Imperfect Single World* after my *Midlife* agent and editor both said they weren't interested. My printing experience included web presses, the type used by newspapers and magazine publishers, and offset presses. I wasn't ready to print a large quantity of books and wondered if there was a cost effective way to print smaller quantities of books.

I searched the Web for printing options and found CafePress, www.cafepress.com. According to their website, they would print one or more copies of my book, from my submitted files, with no upfront costs. I bought a block of ten

ISBNs, produced the book block and cover files to CafePress's specifications, submitted the files for printing, and ordered three copies.

My cost for the 218-page softcover book was over $14, excluding shipping and the cost of an ISBN. When I determined that the list price would have to be over $35 to make even a minimal return, I looked for a more cost effective method.

BookSurge

Amazon.com wasn't always in the print-on-demand business but when they finally figured out there were more profits to be had if they not only *sold* books but also *printed* them, they went right for the jugular, telling publishers using PODs that their softcover books could only be sold through Amazon.com and their affiliates if they were printed through one of Amazon's POD affiliates.

BookSurge, Amazon's first dabble into POD printing, offered a tasty $99 package of services which included complete pre-press editing, layout, and design. In the $99 package, authors got essentially the same services subsidy publishers were charging thousands of dollars for, and some subsidy publishers made easy money being the middleman between BookSurge and new authors.

November 2009, BookSurge merged with CreateSpace.

CreateSpace

At the same time that BookSurge's prices increased, Amazon introduced CreateSpace, a free service that could also funnel business into BookSurge. Recently, CreateSpace has begun offering paid services similar to those offered by BookSurge.

Until early in 2008, I had no reason to use CreateSpace for any of my publishing or printing projects. That changed when Amazon advised POD publishers that their paperback books would have to be printed through CreateSpace or BookSurge to be sold on Amazon.com and its affiliates.

I was already printing my books through Lightning Source and it seemed redundant to duplicate the effort with CreateSpace. However, I didn't want to lose the marketing opportunity provided through the world's largest online bookseller. I also I didn't want to lose potential book sales through the Amazon Affiliates program.

After setting up an account with CreateSpace, I submitted the same PDFs used to print *Advice for an Imperfect Single World* through Lightning Source. Because CreateSpace has no sign-up or membership fees, my cost was around $12 for a proof of my book, most of which included shipping.

I don't know if Amazon still requires POD publishers to use their print-on-demand services. For me, what began as a negative – being pushed into using CreateSpace – had a positive outcome: I use CreateSpace so my books will have Amazon distribution and to print preview or "proof" copies of new books.

I always recommend that self-publishing authors use CreateSpace for the first printing of a book before going the extra steps and expense to publish through Lightning Source. There is no way to get the "feel" of a book's layout and design without having the actual printed and bound book in hand. Using CreateSpace for that first copy is fast and inexpensive since there are no upfront fees to pay.

Even though Mark Levine puts CreateSpace into the category of "Publishers Who Are Just OK" in *The Fine Print of Self Publishing*, I have incorporated CreateSpace into a self-publishing plan that has worked well for me and the authors I've helped self-publish.

Becoming A Publisher

Ambitious authors can set up their own small publishing company and not only self-publish their books but also publish books for other authors although I don't recommend publishing other authors' books before getting significant experience self-publishing.

Most of the information I found about setting up a publishing business focused on being *in* business not the legalities of *setting up* a company. Becoming a publisher isn't just thinking up a unique name, designing a logo, ordering business cards, buying a block of ISBNs, and printing books. Publishing is a business that involves occupational licenses; local, city, county, state and federal taxes; business bank accounts; detailed accounting; perhaps even going after seed money to get started.

I am not a business consultant and I won't offer business advice. I am a business owner and know from being in business for over 25 years that accounting, taxes, legalities, and voluminous paperwork are part and parcel of owning any business.

It is worth repeating: take a simpler route for the first book – printing through CreateSpace – before deciding if it will be worth the extra expense, and stress, to get into the self-publishing business.

Offset Printing

Publishers can print books in large quantities on offset presses or as ordered using print-on-demand (POD) printers. Layout, design, and pre-press costs will be the same whether a book is printed on an offset press or by a POD printer. When the press ready files get to the offset printer, the costs begin adding up.

The biggest cost of running a standard printing press, offset or web, is at startup when the plates are set and test pages are printed. Setup costs are usually a fixed amount whether one book is printed or 200,000.

The cost per book *will* go down the more copies are printed because the initial setup/startup costs will be spread over a larger number of books. But print costs also include overhead (normal costs of doing business, including employee wages, benefits, and insurance), paper, ink, and profit, and there will be a point where the price per copy stabilizes.

Let's say, for example, the cost to print 10,000 books is $10,000, making the per book print cost $1. With a list price of $14.95 and the standard 55% discount to retailers, the net would be $5.73 per book sold ($14.95 - $8.22/discount = $6.73 - $1.00/printing cost = $5.73). But that isn't true net profit because it doesn't factor in the pre-press expenses, warehousing, shipping, marketing and promotions, and normal business expenses.

The upside of printing a large quantity of books is the ability to keep the list price low enough to be competitive. But, there are several downsides, the first of which is the print cost. Paying out several thousand dollars can be daunting regardless of how passionate an author may be about seeing their book in print. The second is the issue of storage, paying for warehousing such a large number of books so they will be safe from mildew, mold, rodents, theft, fire and other damage or loss. And, the the biggest negative for volume printing, in my opinion, is the cost to dispose of thousands of unsold books if it becomes necessary to print corrections, edits, or updates.

Lightning Source POD

After printing *Advice for an Imperfect Single World* through CafePress, at a per copy price of over $14 excluding shipping, I continued to look for a better way to print my books. Then I discovered Lightning Source, www.lightningsource.com.

After reading through the printing and distribution information on the Lightning Source website, I knew they would be my last stop. Printing the same 218-page book through LSI brought my per copy cost down to $5.94 excluding shipping.

Lightning Source is the printer for virtually every publisher doing business today, from major publishing houses to most self-publishing and subsidy publishers. They provide offset printing in addition to print-on-demand (POD) printing.

POD is a relatively new concept and it has its critics, but there is no denying the value of print-on-demand to cut costs for short runs. For quantity printing, offset printing is more cost effective. And, some types of books, such as coffee table and pop-up books, can only be printed on offset presses.

I've seen POD printing criticized as not as good as offset printing but I haven't seen a difference in quality between books I've printed through Lightning Source and CreateSpace and books printed before POD printers existed.

Self-publishing through Lightning Source allows me to make minor revisions to my books which means buyers will receive the most current version of my book. My cost per book is low and I can order as few as one or as many books as I might need for my own use. Environmentally, POD is a good choice since books are not printed until sold which eliminates waste. It also eliminates warehousing costs.

Most importantly, my books are distributed through Lightning Source's distribution partners including Ingram, Amazon.com, Baker & Taylor, Barnes & Noble, NACSCORP, Rittenhouse, and the new Espresso Book Machine. International printing and distribution is also available.

For me, book publishing doesn't get much better than this.

Parts
Of A Book

To uncomplicate what should be between the covers of a book, a book is complete with three elements: Title Page, Copyright Page, and Main Text. Common sense and using current, best-selling, books of the same genre as examples should suggest what else to include.

Books published by major publishing houses follow specific guidelines for book layout and design. Self-publishers can be more flexible with book layout but to appeal to the largest number of readers, it is smart to incorporate basic elements of traditionally published books.

Covers and Binding

The covers of a paperback are straightforward: front, back, and spine. The front cover should have a dynamic design that "sells" the book. The cover should look good as a thumbnail version of itself since that is the way it will appear in most catalogues and online bookseller sites.

The back cover should be a small taste of what's inside and may also include recommendations and comments by others as to why the book is a "must read."

The spine, if the book is thick enough, will include title, author's name, and publisher's name or logo. The spine is extremely important since most books in bookstores and bookcases are positioned spine out.

Wrappers of clothbound hardcover books have front and back flaps with room for author information and short excerpts. Underneath the wrapper, the cloth cover will usually have the title imprinted in simple text on the front cover and spine.

The cover on a gloss laminate hardcover book is the same as the cover of a paperback book.

The Book Block

The book block consists of front matter, text block, and back matter. The front matter has several elements, some standard, depending upon the type of book being published. Back matter may not be necessary for a work of fiction but in non-fiction books it contains key, expected, elements.

Front Matter

The following pages comprise the front matter of a book. Rarely will all pages be included in a book nor must the order be as described. At a minimum, I believe the front matter should have a Title page and a Copyright page.

Half Title Page: The first right hand printed page in most books by traditional publishing houses will be a page with just the title, nothing more, sometimes in the same font as on the front cover. I usually break the rules by including the subtitle.

Series Title Page: Authors with previous published books would list them in chronological order on the back of the half title page. The usual way to list other published book(s) is centered, by title, under "Also by (author name)." Subtitles may also be included.

Title Page: The Title page is the second right hand page after the half title page. This page includes the full book title and subtitle (if any), sometimes in the same font as on the front cover. It also includes author's name and any coauthors, editors, or illustrators listed on the front cover. The publisher's logo and name are at the bottom of the page.

Copyright Page: The Copyright page is on the reverse side of the title page and the only other page that should absolutely be included in the front matter. Information on this page would include: publisher name and location, copyright information, edition date, ISBN, PCN, disclaimer, and where printed. This page may also contain permissions and acknowledgements. If these are substantial, they may be moved to pages of their own.

Dedication Page: The Dedication page is a right hand page opposite the copyright page or elsewhere in the front matter. A book does not need a dedication nor is the wording "Dedicated to" used, just a simple "For so-and-so." The reverse of the dedication page is blank.

Epigraph: The Epigraph is also on a right hand page. It would be a quote or phrase pertaining to the book's subject matter. The epigraph for this book is a public domain quotation by Jules Renard. Quotes by living persons, not in public domain, require their permission.

Table of Contents: Non-fiction books usually have a table of contents and fiction books may have a table of contents if chapters are unique or the book is a compilation of various works. The table of contents listing can be simple, with just the main chapters listed, or complex, with sub-chapters and descriptions under each entry or sub-entry. Chapter and section headings should match the table of contents listings and page numbers must be correct.

List of Illustrations: When a book contains artwork or photographs by several sources or contributors, a List of Illustrations page is appropriate. This is another right hand page, generally placed after the table of contents. The listings would include title and/or description of each illustration or photograph and the page number each appears on.

Preface: The Preface, another right hand page, summarizes the author's reason for writing the book, his or her research methods, and may include acknowledgements of other persons were instrumental in getting the book to completion.

Foreword: Commonly found in nonfiction books, the foreword is written by someone other than the author who is known as an expert in the field or topic covered by the book.

Acknowledgments Page: Generally there is no need for an Acknowledgements page if a Preface page is used as both serve the same purpose. One or the other is used by authors to name and thank people who may have provided help and support during the writing and/or publishing process.

Book Block Text

There are several elements that can be a part of this middle section but only the main text is necessary for a book to actually *be* a book. Most non-fiction books will contain several of the following elements; some fiction books will have only the main text.

Introduction: The Introduction prepares the reader for what is to come. In fiction, this could be a bit of the history of the characters or a short description leading up to when the current story begins, particularly if the book is part of a series. In nonfiction books, the introduction may give details about research or things the author wants the reader to keep in mind while reading the book.

Main Text/Chapters/Parts: Books can be divided into sections and then divided further into sub-sections. This usually would occur in a nonfiction book although complex novels may have multiple divisions and sub-sections. A book should have as many sections or chapters as necessary so that the material flows properly.

Epilogue/Afterword: The Epilogue tells the reader what happened to the main characters after the story ended and the Afterword can give readers a mini synopsis of what they've just read or provide advice to help readers better use the material.

Conclusion: The Conclusion may be in place of, or in addition to, the Epilogue or Afterword and it may or may not be numbered as the final chapter of the book.

Back Matter

The following are commonly found in the back matter of a book with non-fiction books usually having more back matter sections. None of the following sections are required and there is no specific order in which they appear although some sections would, logically, be placed before others.

Appendix: The Appendix contains resources, references, checklists, and other items that will be useful to the reader.

Glossary: The Glossary would list, alphabetically with definitions, words and phrases that are not typically used by the average reader including Web slang and texting abbreviations. Non-fiction books of a technical nature usually contain a glossary and fiction books of certain genres (science fiction, for example) may also include a glossary.

Index: The Index is standard in many non-fiction books. It lists key words and phrases found throughout the book, and the page numbers they appear on. It is not important to list every page that a key word or phrase appears on, only those pages that actually contain relevant information regarding the particular word or phrase.

References or Bibliography: The References or Bibliography pages list books and other reference sources and materials used by the author. According to the *Chicago Manual of Style,* the proper way to list reference sources is alphabetically by the author's last name, year published, and the publication title.

Resources: A Resources section would include books, Web sites, organizations, associations, newsletters, and other resources pertainent to the book's topic.

Notes: Non-fiction books are more likely to have a Notes section, arranged by chapter, with details that would have bogged down the flow of the book.

Colophon: If included, the Colophon is usually in the back matter although some publishers include it in the front matter. Information in the colophon is probably of more interest to publishers, typographers, and printers. The colophon details the production of the book including the type of printing press, typography information, person(s) who did the pre-press work, software programs used, and specifics as to paper, binding and cover.

About the Author: While some of the previous sections might seem unnecessary, in my opinion, the About the Author page is very important. Some authors place this information closer to the main text. I usually put it just in front of pages with details about one or more of my other books.

The About the Author page should include a short biography of the author(s), areas of expertise, other books by the author(s), a few personal details, and a photo. If author details are included on the back cover of the book, they can be rewritten for this page.

Order Form: Some publishers and authors include an Order Form to make it easier for readers to order additional copies of the current book, or copies of other of the author's or publisher's books. The page might be a fill-in tear-out form that can be completed and faxed or mailed.

Upcoming and Other Books: Instead of leaving the last few pages of a book blank, the Upcoming and Other Books page is an additional marketing opportunity for authors or publishers with more than one published book. I make sure that I have enough blank pages to promote several of my books.

Preparing
To Publish

Authors have two options to get from manuscript to published book: contract with a publisher, or *be* the publisher. Each has advantages and disadvantages.

If an author contracts with a publisher, their control over the book's design and layout will depend upon the publisher. If the book ends up winning awards, the publishing house will be the one to receive the notariety and profits.

A publisher such as CreateSpace prints what the author provides. Some subsidy publishers will accept author input as long as the author's checkbook is open. Major publishing houses will listen to an author's concerns but their staff will usually have the final word.

Self-published or not, all authors will be concerned with:

Cover Design – Never discount the importance of a well-designed book cover. The cover is the first, and sometimes primary, marketing tool.

Typesetting and Layout – If a potential buyer is intrigued enough by a book's cover to take a look inside, they shouldn't be disappointed with poor page design and typography.

Copyright – A book is actually copyright protected once the words are put on paper. When the book is published, the copyright can be registered online by visiting www.loc.gov/copyright/.

Self-publishers have additional work to do:

ISBN – The International Standard Book Number (ISBN), issued to publishers, is used by distributors and retailers to identify the publisher, title, and the binding of the specific publication. As an example, a search on Amazon.com for ISBN 978-0-9761210-8-4 goes directly to the paperback version of *Teen Mom: A Journal*. That ISBN will never be associated with another title or another version of this title.

A book needs an ISBN so it can be sold by retailers. ISBNs for books published in the U.S. are available through R.R. Bowker (www.bowkerlink.com). ISBNs issued through Bowker are a 13-digit format which includes the EAN "country" prefix of 978 for "Bookland."

Each 13-digit ISBN has a corresponding 10-digit ISBN which may also be included on the copyright page. The 10-digit ISBN has similar but not identical numbers so just deleting the 978 prefix from a 13-digit ISBN does not produce the matching 10-digit ISBN.

SAN – The Standard Address Number is a seven-digit number that can be requested at the same time a publisher applies for ISBNs. SANs are assigned to publishers, bookstores, distributors, wholesalers, libraries, schools, and book manufacturers. The SAN is a unique number used to identify a specific address such as a billing address or one for placing orders. Each address would have a separate SAN.

The SAN is *not* printed on the copyright page, it is used on letterhead, invoices, and other correspondence. SANs are also searchable by subscribers to BookIndustryLocator.com. Each SAN requested has a non-refundable one time service charge of $150. When I bought my first block of ISBNs I did get a SAN although I rarely use it.

Bar Code – Publishers need to obtain bar code art for the bottom right-hand corner of the book's back cover. Bar codes are available, for various prices, through Bowker Bar Code Service and other online sites. If publishing through Lightning Source, their free Cover Generator can be used to create a cover template with bar code already in place. CreateSpace will add a bar code, without cost.

The Bookland EAN bar code actually is a set of two bar codes. The bar code on the left is the ISBN EAN. The bar code to the right is a 5-digit, EAN-5, which is the retail price of the publication. The first digit is the currency. For US dollars, the digit is a 5. So, digits of 51495 would mean the retail price of the book is $14.95. Bar codes without the price encoded display a default null code of 90000. If there the price of the book might be changed in the future, it's better to use the 90000 null code on the bar code.

PCN/LCCN – Publishers should apply to the Library of Congress, www.loc.gov, for a Preassigned Control Number before publishing so the LLCN – Library of Congress Control Number – can be included on the copyright page. Not all books will qualify for the PCN/LCCN but there is no cost to apply.

Unlike the requirement for one ISBN per each version of a title, one LCCN is used for all versions of the same title.

Book Layout
Using Microsoft Word

This book is a work in progress. It is being written as I work through the self-publishing process so I can write about the steps as I go along.

I learned typesetting and layout when an economic downturn in the late 1980s forced my former husband and I to cut staff and run our small magazine publishing business ourselves.

When I joined the business, layout was done the old-fashioned way – pasting type and graphics to layout boards. Handwritten and typewritten text was sent to an independent typesetter who retyped and set the text into the typefaces, sizes, and column widths our graphic artists needed. When the rolls of typeset text were returned, they were reviewed for errors, sent back for corrections, reviewed again, occasionally returned for more corrections, and finally pasted to the layout boards.

When we decided that our profits were going to subcontractors for work we should be able to do ourselves, we bought several of the first IBM System 2 PCs, installed Adobe's earliest versions of Photoshop and Pagemaker, and our artists learned desktop publishing "on the job."

At the same time, I used WordPerfect to write editorials, copied the text files onto floppy disks, and gave them to the art staff for insertion into their Pagemaker layouts. I decided that it could save more time and effort if I could set the type into the pages and I, too, learned to work with Pagemaker.

By the time the economy took a deep dip and we were forced to let our employees go, I was able to do the pre-press work necessary to keep the business going.

I give this little bit of history because it is second nature to me to do book layout in Pagemaker even though it is a fairly complex (and expensive) software program. I've been using it for over 20 years so I *should* be fairly proficient by now. I also learned to use an early version of QuarkXPress while working part-time for a newspaper more than 15 years ago.

Most authors don't need to be proficient with Pagemaker, QuarkXPress, InDesign, or Photoshop. They aren't in the *publishing* business, they're in the *writing* business. They do what they do best — write — and pay others to do what *they* do best — layout and design. Until now, that is.

Using online resources, it is possible for anyone to design a good book cover as I'll demonstrate in an upcoming chapter. As far as interior page layout, Microsoft Word does a decent job. The biggest flaw I find using Word is the ease in which Word creates new type styles.

When Gordon Ratcliff asked me to help him self-publish his first novel, *The Judas Fragment*, he gave me a CD containing his manuscript in a Word document over 600 pages in length. I don't know any writers who don't try to do at least some page layout as they write and Gordon was no exception.

Even though text throughout the document *appeared* to be the same style, it wasn't. When I changed the font for body text, random portions of the document reflected the change. I also discovered that some paragraph indents were created using the space bar instead of setting tabs, and spacing between sentences was not uniform.

In order to standardize the body text to just one style, I deleted all of the text styles in use. Text formatted with a deleted style reverted to the default style. Once all the styles had been deleted, I made changes to the default style to see which typefaces, sizes, and spacing worked best.

At more than 600 pages, the novel was unwieldy in size, and would be expensive to print – even using CreateSpace. This meant the retail price would have be higher than comparative books. The page count came down using smaller body text and narrower margins, but only heavy editing brought the final page count to just over 400 pages.

When I receive a Word document for layout, I usually save it as a plain text file (.txt), search for odd spacing and other issues, and then import it into Pagemaker. In Pagemaker I format the entire text using one body text style. Then, page by page, I make style changes to headings, subheads, captions, and selected text.

For this book, I wanted to find a program that worked with Word that would provide a book template or otherwise simplify the layout process. I searched the Web and found a program called Book Design Wizard that works inside of Word, and is available for download through Self-Pub.net. After paying for the program ($40 in August 2009), I downloaded and installed it on my computer.

Before opening Book Design Wizard, I copied and pasted blog posts from my self-publishing blog to new Word documents which I saved as plain text files to remove all hidden formatting picked up during the copy and paste process.

Converting to a plain text file doesn't show every flaw in a manuscript, such as indents made by multiple hits on the spacebar, or text that has been centered the same way. But, it is easier to go through the text manuscript to find problems and correct them with "Search & Replace" before importing the file into Pagemaker or, in this case, Book Design Wizard. I do several searches for double spaces and replace all with single spaces until all double spaces have been replaced.

Using Book Design Wizard with Microsoft Word

Once Book Design Wizard is installed on my computer, I select "New Word Document" from my Windows Start menu. Microsoft Word's New Document Wizard now has a new tab for "Book Design Wizard."

I click on the tab and then on the new document icon and a page opens to the Book Design Wizard.

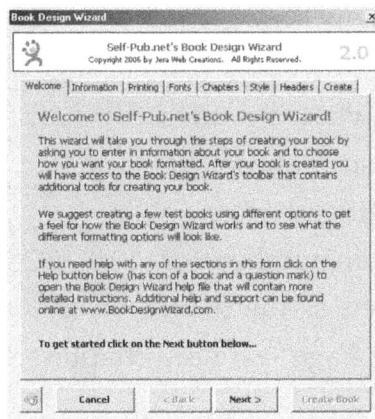

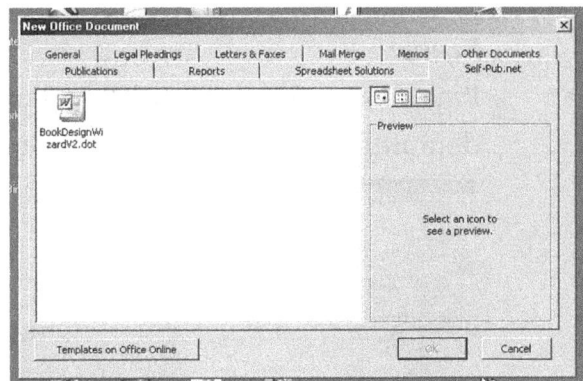

Book Information

Title: How To Be A Self-Published Author

Subtitle: A Step-By-Step Guide

Author: Pat Gaudette

ISBN: 978-09825617-0-6

Check to Include in Book: I'm not sure which items I will need but feel it is better to select most or all of the pages listed and delete the unused ones later.

Printing

I select Professional Printer and then enter the width and height for the page size. My original choice is 7 by 10, which I later change to 8.25 by 8.25, then 6 by 9, and finally 8 by 10. I wanted to use a wider page size of 10 by 8 but it is not a standard size offered by CreateSpace or Lightning Source.

Fonts

I'm not sure which fonts I'll end up using so I keep the default fonts, Arial and Garamond which the Wizard finds on my computer.

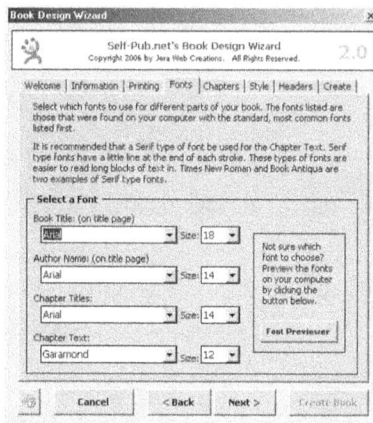

Chapter Titles

I don't know how many chapters this book will have or what the titles will be so I enter the chapter titles I have so far and then numbers for future chapters which will be updated as the book progresses. I select "Next Right Side Page" so new chapters start on right hand pages.

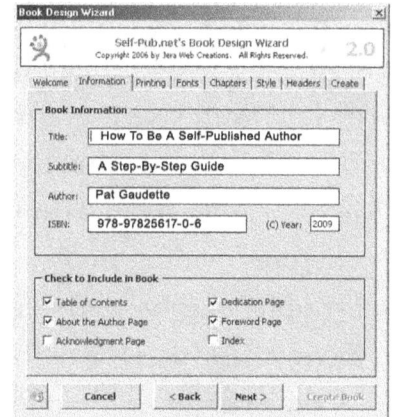

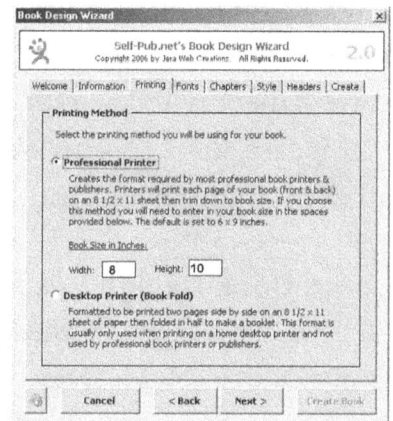

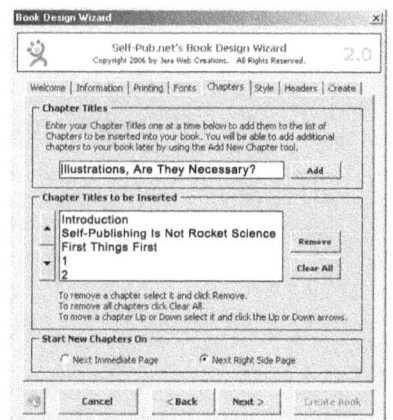

Style

For Chapter Titles I select: Alignment–Left; Space Before–42; Bottom Border–Yes; Character Spacing–None.

For Chapter Paragraphs I select Indent First Line By–1/4 inch; and Line Spacing–Double.

Mousing over the dropdown box for each style shows me the various options available.

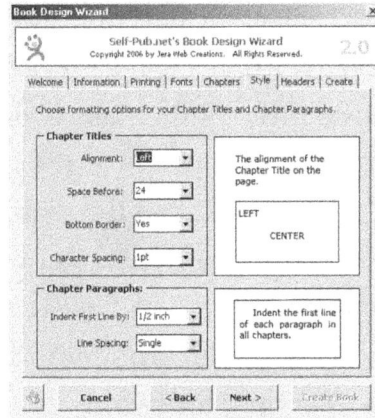

Headers

For the Left Header I select "Current Chapter Title" from the dropdown box, and "Book Title" for the Right Header. I select Bottom of Page (Outside Edges) for Page Numbers. The dropdown boxes show all available options and examples of all options are displayed next to the choices available.

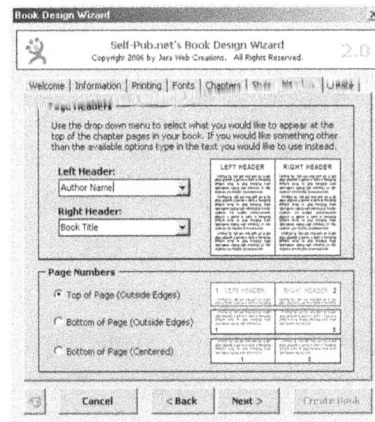

Create Book

Once I finish entering information and making my selections, I'm at Create Page where I click "Create Book" at the bottom.

My newly created book document has a Title page, Copyright page, Foreword, Table of Contents with the chapter headings I've listed so far, and individual pages with my chapter headings. All I need to do now is add text to the pages.

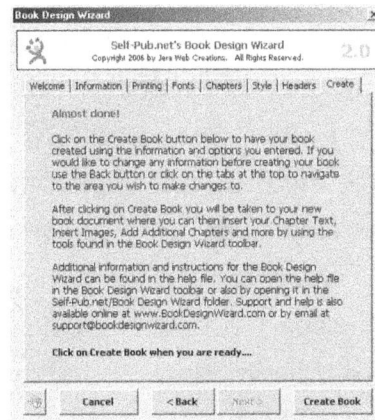

Adding Text

To add the text to the first chapter, I double click at [Double Click To Add Text]. Double clicking brings up a choice of three ways to add text: paste text and strip original formatting; paste text and keep original formatting; type or insert the text manually.

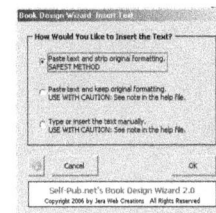

I select the first option, click OK, and find the first "flaw" – I should have copied the text to be pasted before clicking OK. Because I had not done this, text I copied earlier for another task is pasted to the page. When I copy the chapter text from my blog and paste it over the incorrect text, it corrupts the formatting on the page.

In a quick read through the Help files, I find a caution that the first paragraph of each chapter contains important formatting for the entire document. The formatting was deleted when I pasted the new copy over the incorrect text and I'm not sure how to get the original formatting back.

For chapter two, I copy the chapter text first, then double click, select the first option, click OK, and the properly formatted text is pasted to the document.

The Book Design Wizard toolbar is at the upper left of the screen and clicking the "v" provides dropdown selections to choose from. None of the selections are options that will correct the formatting in the first chapter, nor does a search of the more comprehensive Help section give the information I need. I delete chapter one entirely.

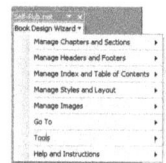

After adding text to some of the chapters, I decide to change the page style and select "Manage Styles and Layout" from the Wizard toolbar, then "Change Book Margins" to change the default settings for Top, Bottom, Left and Right to 1 inch and change the Gutter to 0.5 from 0.25. After a couple more chapters, I change the page size from 7 by 10 to 8.25 by 8.25 and add more space to the margins. Each change is immediately reflected in the layout.

I found layout with Microsoft Word to be somewhat difficult because I rarely use the program. Someone more proficient with Word might not experience the various "glitches" I did while using Word and Book Design Wizard.

Spacing between paragraphs was not always consistent and removing an extra line space occasionally deleted text in the line above. I also noticed that the cursor would sometimes move up or down one line and new text would either show up where I intended it to be or on the line the cursor moved to.

When I used Word's format tool to make a single word bold or italicized within a paragraph, text in the entire manuscript would change to bold or italicized. The first time this happened, I deleted the book file, and started over. The second time, determined to find a better fix than starting over, I went to Edit on the Word toolbar and clicked "Don't automatically update text." All text except what I had bolded reverted back to the original style.

Inserting images was a little tricky, and moving images to a position other than the middle of the page required first clicking on the image, then clicking on Text Wrap in the image editing toolbar. Selecting the option "Edit Wrap Points" allowed the image to be moved elsewhere on the page. It wasn't necessary to set any text wrap options to move the image.

Another image mistake happened when I inserted images just after chapter subtitles. Because the image insertion was linked to the subtitle, the image itself became a part of the subtitle. Even though the page appeared normal, the image was included in the Table of Contents below the subtitle to which it was linked.

Once I realized why the images were showing up in the Table of Contents, I deleted the images, chose a new insertion point – at the beginning of the first paragraph after the subtitle – then reinserted the image.

I highly recommend becoming thoroughly familiar with Book Design Wizard's Help section before starting a book project. Even then there may be some things that aren't covered or aren't obvious.

Converting to PDF

One task that wasn't explained was how to convert the completed Book Design Wizard file to a PDF, the final and very important step to making the document ready for the printer. There were no instructions that this step had to be done, nothing in the expanded Help, nor could I find details in the Help section of the website.

The best program for creating PDF files is Adobe Acrobat and while the price for the most current version might be high for infrequent use, a search of Amazon.com found older versions of Acrobat, new in the box, priced under $100.

Adobe Acrobat isn't the only PDF maker that can be used but it is the best. A web search for "free pdf converter" brings up a long list of products and online services. Because a new PDF file will have to be created each time the book block is revised, purchasing a program such as Adobe Acrobat, even an earlier version, is a good investment because it will be used multiple times during the self-publishing process.

Because I have Adobe Acrobat 9 installed on my computer, I expected to click on the Acrobat icon in Word and create a PDF of the book file but the Book Design Wizard toolbar opened instead. When I removed Book Design Wizard from the completed book document file — an option through the Wizard toolbar — I was then able to use Acrobat to create a PDF file.

Microsoft Word 2007 can save files as PDFs with the PDF add-in downloadable from the Microsoft.com website. There are limited options with this add-in and it changes the dpi of images in the documents which is okay for some documents but not for PDFs that will be uploaded to CreateSpace or Lightning Source as both require image resolution to be 300 dpi or higher.

CreateSpace does not do book layout nor do they correct errors. They print what an author provides to them, misspellings, grammatical errors, poor layout, and all. What they get is what you'll get back except it will be printed, bound, and for sale at Amazon.com and other retailers.

I did the first layout of this book in Word and Book Design Wizard so I could understand and describe the process. While I think Word by itself, or with Book Design Wizard, will produce a good book layout, I did the final layout in Adobe Pagemaker, a program I'm more experienced using.

Authors submitting digital copies of manuscripts to major publishing houses, should submit them as unformatted Word documents. Self-publishing authors hiring others to do the typography and layout, should do the same. A formatted document, while pleasant to the author's eye, adds time and money to the pre-press work done on a book.

Suggested Reading: *Perfect Pages,* by Aaron Shepard, explains in detail how to use Word to prepare a book for print-on-demand publishing.

CreateSpace
www.CreateSpace.com

CreateSpace functions as either a publisher or a printer. If their ISBN is used on a book, they are the publisher. If a publisher's ISBN is used on a book, CreateSpace is the printer. There is no difference in the file submission process, print costs, or title set-up.

Before setting up a book through CreateSpace, it is necessary to first set up an account. There is no cost involved to set up an account or submit files, and credit card information won't be necessary until a proof copy is ready for review. When royalty payments are due to be paid, banking information will be required if payments are to be direct deposited.

After setting up an account, log into the Member Dashboard and bookmark it for quick access. This is my Member Dashboard prior to adding this book:

To set up a book, click the Add New Title button. This opens up a page listing various products to select from: DVD on-Demand, Audio CD, Audio Download, or Paperback Book.

To set up this book, I click Paperback Book and the Title Setup page opens.

Films, TV Shows, Documentaries, and more

DVD on-Demand
Professional-quality DVDs, created and shipped on-demand. More Info...

Video Download
Distribute your title through Amazon's Video On Demand service. More Info...

Music, Spoken Word, Lectures, and more

Audio CD
Professional-quality Audio CDs, created and shipped on-demand. More Info...

Audio Download
Distribute your title through Amazon MP3. More Info...

Novels, Nonfiction, Poetry, Children's Books, and more

Paperback Book
Your book, professionally printed, bound, and shipped on-demand. More Info...

Title Setup

Blocks on each page of the set-up that must be completed in order to save the page and continue to the next are marked with a red *. The other information can be filled in later and most of the information can be revised at a later time except where indicated.

* Title: How to be a Self-Published Author

Subtitle: A Step-by-Step Guide

Volume Number: 1

* Description: Self-publishing is not rocket science. Today's technology makes it simple for authors who are fairly computer savvy to also self publish. This guide, written by a publishing consultant and self-published author, is for authors who are tired of waiting for someone else to publish their books.

* **Title**	How to be a Self-Published Author
	This cannot be changed after you submit this book for publishing.
Subtitle	A Step-by-Step Guide
	This cannot be changed after you submit this book for publishing.
Volume Number	1
	This cannot be changed after you submit this book for publishing.
* **Description** about the description...	Self-publishing is not rocket science. Today's technology makes it simple for authors who are fairly computer savvy to also self publish. This guide, written by a publishing consultant and self-published author, is for authors who are tired of waiting for someone else to publish their book.

You may enter a maximum of 2,000 characters in book description field.

* ISBN: The ISBN provides information about the book publisher to wholesalers and retailers. I am using my ISBN so my company will be identified as the publisher. If CreateSpace was going to be the publisher, I would check "Assign my book an ISBN-13/EAN-13 immediately." *Note: once completed, this cannot be changed!*

Imprint Name: Home & Leisure Publishing, Inc.

BISAC Category: In the left column I select Reference and then to narrow it down, I choose Writing Skills from the right column. I click "Add Selected" so the category selection will be saved otherwise I will get an error when I try to submit the completed page.

Reading Level: I usually select Tenth Grade for my books. If I was writing something appropriate for a different demographic, such as college graduates, the reading level selection would reflect that.

---

* ISBN
what's this?

○ Assign my book an ISBN-13/EAN-13 immediately.
IMPORTANT: If you select this option, an ISBN-13/EAN-13 will be immediately assigned to your book upon clicking the Save & Continue button at the bottom of this page. Once the page has been saved, the selection cannot be changed.

○ I already own an ISBN-10 for this book.

> 0982561709

This cannot be changed after you submit this book for publishing.

⊙ I already own an ISBN-13/EAN-13 for this book.

> 9780982561706

This cannot be changed after you submit this book for publishing.
If you have an ISBN that you purchased from R.R. Bowker or the International ISBN agency specifically for this book, you may use it in publishing your book through our tool. Please note you will be required to also enter an imprint (or publisher) name and that we will verify the ownership and authenticity of the ISBN you enter.

Imprint Name
what's this?

> Home & Leisure Publishing, Inc.

This cannot be changed after you submit this book for publishing.

BISAC Category
what's this?

Enter BISAC Category Code

Reference >	Quotations
Religion >	Research
Science >	Thesauri
Self-Help >	Trivia
Social Science >	Weddings
Sports & Recreation >	Word Lists
Study Aids >	Writing Skills
Technology & Engineering >	Yearbooks & Annuals
Transportation >	

* Selected Categories

> Reference / Writing Skills

Reading Level

> Tenth Grade

This book previously published on: Not previously published.

Country of Publication: United States.

Publication Date: I have to leave this blank. The program won't accept a future date and gave me an error message when I entered my expected publication date.

Language: English.

Search Keywords: publishing, self publisher, how to publish a book, getting published.

Authored by: Pat Gaudette (This must be exactly how the name will appear on the cover.)

Author's Biography: I'll complete this section later. This is an important section because what appears here will also appear on Amazon.com and may be picked up by other affiliate sites.

Save & Continue

This book previously published on	Not previously published
Country of Publication	United States
Publication Date	Month Day Year
	We will automatically assign the publication date for your book when your file is approved for publishing unless you specify one here.
	This cannot be changed after you submit this book for publishing.
Language	English
	Choose primary language
Search Keywords about search keywords...	publishing,how to publish a book,self-publisher,getting published

Contributors
about entering contributors...

    * **Authored By**   Author's name must appear on your book's cover

	Pat		Gaudette	
Prefix	First Name / Initial	Middle Name / Initial	Last Name / Surname*	Suffix

Author's Biography
where does this appear?

You may enter a maximum of 2,500 characters in the author biography field.

This cannot be changed after you submit this book for publishing.

Physical Properties

In order to move on to the pages after this one, all the information on the Physical Properties page must be completed. This information can be changed later, before the book is submitted for publishing, but future changes will also affect cover layout, pricing, and royalty share. Changes cannot be made after the book is published.

* **Number of Pages:** I don't know what the final page count will be but 104 is a good number for now.

* **Interior Type:** I choose Black and White which means all text and images won't extend past the trim zone. If I intended to place images closer to the edge of the page and even beyond the page trim marks, I would choose Black and White with Bleed. This would alert CreateSpace that placing an image in the trim zone was by design, not by mistake.

* **Trim Size:** After trying various page sizes for this book, I've decided to use a larger page format of 8" x 10".

Binding: Already pre-selected as US Trade Paper.

* **Paper Color:** I originally planned on using cream paper because it is slightly heavier but Lightning Source does not offer cream for their 8x10 page size. Since I am using the same files to print this book through Lightning Source and CreateSpace, I choose White so I can compare print quality.

Save & Continue

* **Number of Pages** about page count...	104 Page count must be an even number.
* **Interior Type**	Black and White Bleed is extra image or background that extends beyond the trim marks of a page.
* **Trim Size** what's this?	8" x 10"
Binding	US Trade Paper
* **Paper Color**	White

These fields cannot be changed after you submit this book for publishing.

Back	Save & Continue

Add Files

Once the Interior has been completed and changed to a PDF file this is the page where it would be uploaded to CreateSpace. This is also the page that any revised files would be uploaded.

The information on this page is automatically updated each time I change values on the Physical Properties page. The current messages include my ISBNs and: *According to the interior type and page count you specified on the Physical Properties page, your book's spine width is 0.26 inches.*

I can't upload a PDF for the interior files yet so I skip over the Book Interior section and click on the Easy option, Create a Cover, in the Book Cover section.

Add your interior and cover files.

According to the interior type and page count you specified on the Physical Properties page, your book's spine width is 0.26 inches.

Your book's ISBN is 0982561709 and EAN-13 is 9780982561706.

Download Cover Template

ZIP

Begin download
2mb Compressed Zip File

This Zip file contains

Adobe® Photoshop Template, PNG Template and instructions.

Book Interior

You do not currently have an interior file.

| Upload a PDF |

Format your own book interior file. Read our PDF Submission Requirements.

Book Cover

You do not currently have a cover file.

Easy | Create a Cover | BETA

Start with one of our professional designs, and then customize your cover using this easy online tool.

Advanced | Upload a PDF |

Use our template to create your own cover from scratch. Start by downloading the template.

| Back | | Save & Continue |

Cover Creator

Cover Creator opens in another window and loads a selection of cover templates for an 8" X 10" book. The templates are named for trees and without spine text. I close Cover Creator, go back to Physical Properties, change the page number to 124, save, re-open Cover Creator, and still no spine text. When I change the page count to 134, the templates include spine text.

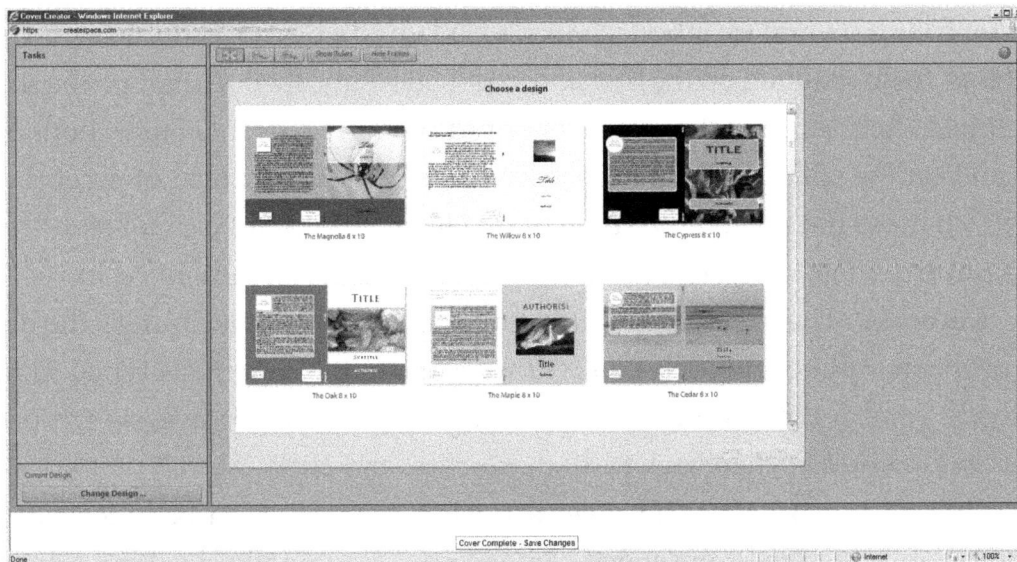

Double clicking on The Oak thumbnail opens up a cover complete with my title, subtitle, and name on the front, the title and my name on the spine, and nonsense text on the back. To the left are the formatting options for the cover.

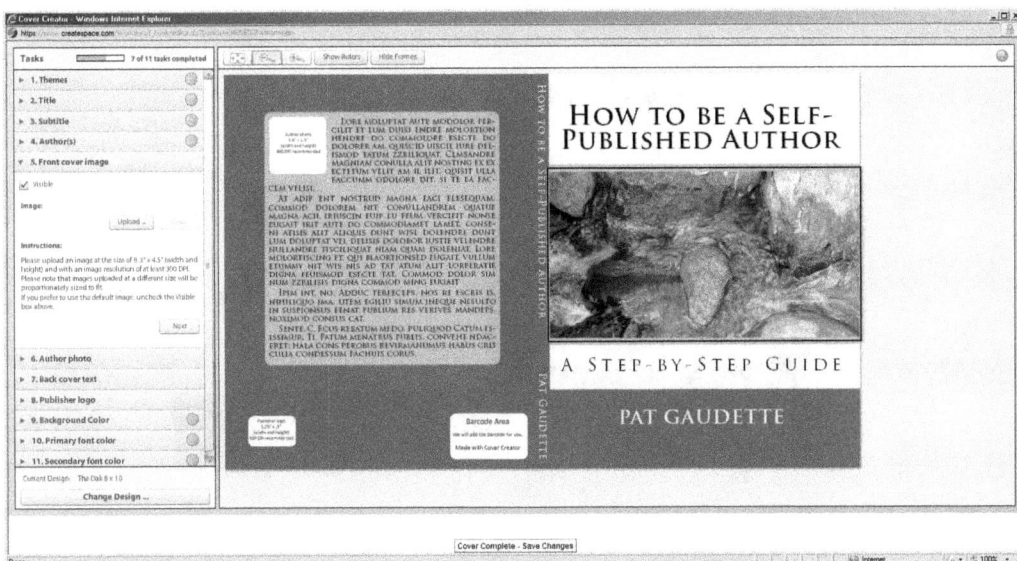

1. Themes: Choosing a different option from the drop down box changes the cover fonts. I choose Solid Poplar, a nice strong font which will still be very readable when the cover is reduced to a thumbnail version.

2 - Title: The book title is already typed in the edit block, in upper and lowercase. The title can be changed so it is all uppercase, some words all uppercase, as well as divided into two lines between specific words.

After trying several variations, I decide on How To Be A Self-Published Author, with How To Be centered on the first line and A Self-Published Author on the second. Each time I click "Apply" the cover is revised with my current choice, both on the front and on the spine. Splitting the title where I want it, instead of accepting the default, changes the title on the spine to two lines of extremely small text.

3 - Subtitle: The subtitle, "A Step-by-Step Guide," is already filled in.

4 - Author(s): The font size is a little larger than I would like but it's the default size for this template and style so I will work with it. My name is typed in upper and lower case in the edit block and I change it to all uppercase, switch back to upper and lowercase, then back to all uppercase, and click "Next."

5 – Front Cover Image: The cover art or photograph must be at least 300 dpi resolution and sized to fit the specific image area. I originally sized my artwork to fit a smaller area and when I upload it for this larger cover, Cover Creator resized the art to fit the larger space resulting in a lower resolution and an error message. Once I resized the artwork to fit the larger area, the error message went away.

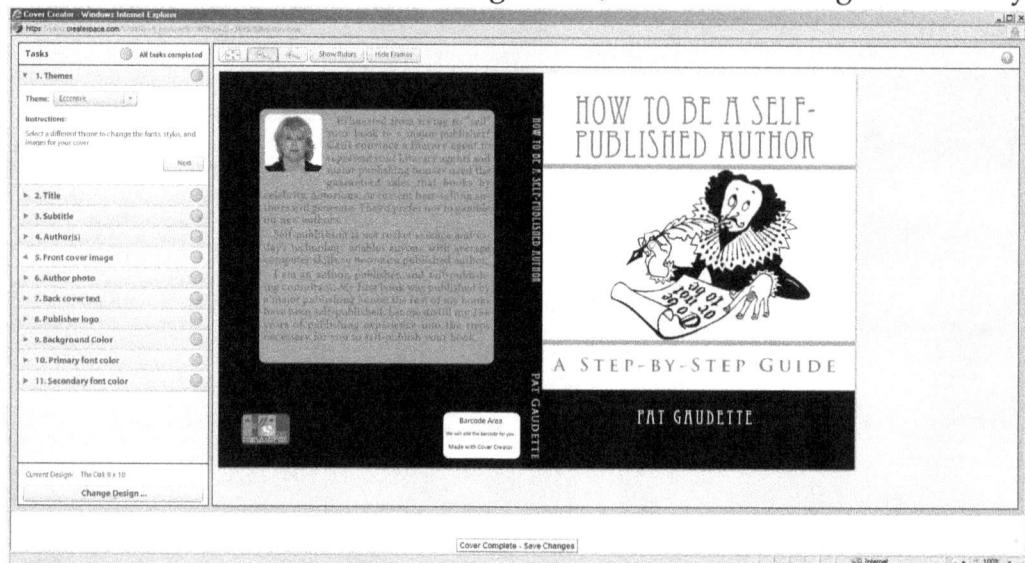

6 - Author Photo: I use Photoshop to resize one of my photos to 1.5"x1.5" and 300 dpi, then save it as a .jpg and also as a .png. When I click Upload and locate the directory on my computer where the photos are saved, the .jpg file is the only one that's visible which means Cover Creator won't accept a .png image. I upload the photo, ignore Cover Creator's Alignment & Rotation tools, and click "Next."

7 - Back cover text: I replace the gibberish text in the box with paragraphs about the book, edit and re-edit until I'm satisfied with the wording, and click "Next."

8 - Publisher Logo: After resizing one of my logos, I upload it to the space provided. I always uncheck the box when using a CreateSpace ISBN so their logo, by default, won't appear on the back cover.

9 - Background Color: Changing the background color is simple with Cover Creator's color picker and after trying various bold colors – Forest Green, Indigo Sky, Hunter Green – I choose Rich Black and click "Next."

10 - Font color: Using the color picker, I try various colors to see which will show up best in the white portion of the front cover. Brick Red seems the best choice for the title and subtitle. The same color also applies to the back cover text.

Again using the color picker, I choose the palest cream for the secondary font color. This is for the author name which appears in the black area of the front cover.

After taking a final look through the various steps, I click "Cover Complete - Save Changes" at the bottom of the window and wait for Cover Creator to save my file and close.

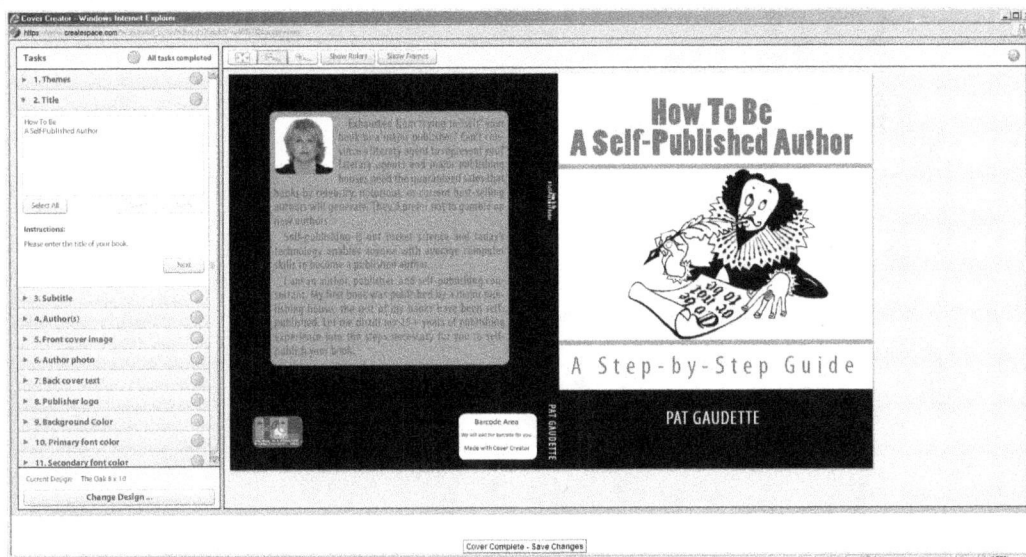

Once it does, a thumbnail of my cover shows up on the Add Files page along with an "Edit Cover" link and "Full Size Preview" link.

I click "Save Changes" to move to the next option and get error messages: *"Please fix the problems noted in red below."* and *"An interior is required."* I'm not ready to upload the interior files and ignore the messages.

→ **Please fix the problems noted in red below.**

Add your interior and cover files.

According to the interior type and page count you specified on the Physical Properties page, your book's spine width is 0.34 inches.

Your book's ISBN is 0982561709 and EAN 13 is 9780982561706.

Download Cover Template

ZIP

Begin download
2mb Compressed Zip File

This Zip file contains

Adobe® Photoshop Template, PNG Template and instructions.

Book Interior

→ **You do not currently have an interior file.**
An interior is required

Upload a PDF

Format your own book interior file. Read our PDF Submission Requirements.

Book Cover

Added by using Cover Creator

✎ Edit Cover

🔍 Full Size Preview

Added by using Cover Cr...

Replace Book Cover
This will remove your existing file and replace it with a new file.

Easy   Create a Cover   BETA

Start with one of our professional designs, and then customize your cover using this easy online tool.

Advanced   Upload a PDF

Use our template to create your own cover from scratch. Start by downloading the template.

Back   Save Changes

Sales & Promotion

Curious as to the cost to publish the book in full color, I go to the top of the page and click Physical Properties then select Full Color With Bleed for the interior pages, save, and then click Sales & Promotion.

Printing this book in full color means the List price must be $23.72 or higher so I enter $23.72 in the List Price block and click Update Royalties. Under CreateSpace's Standard Plan, each book sold on Amazon.com, listed at $23.72, would net a Retail Royalty to me of $0.00 after CreateSpace takes $23.72. I can, however, upgrade to the Pro Plan (for $39) and then my Royalty would be $6.10 per book sold on Amazon.com.

My Royalty is better if I sell a book through my free CreateSpace E-Store. I'll get $4.74 under the Standard Plan and $10.84 under the Pro Plan for each book sold at $23.72 List Price. My cost to order multiple copies is $14.23 per copy under the Standard Plan and $8.13 under the Pro Plan.

It makes little sense to set the List Price at the share paid to CreateSpace so I change the list price to $29.95, which I think is prohibitively high. My cost to order copies stays the same, everything else changes: CreateSpace gets $26.21 Standard and $20.11 Pro; I get $3.74 Standard and $9.84 Pro. In the E-Store I'll get $9.73 Standard and $15.83 Pro.

I return to Physical Properties and change the Interior Type back to Black & White. Changing the Physical Properties causes problems with the cover and I end up with warnings that the book cover needs to be edited to fit the new physical properties of the book — which are now back to what they were when I created the cover.

Ignoring the cover error message, I return to the Sales & Promotion page to make sure my change to Black & White interior pages is reflected and it is. The minimum retail price is shown at $6.10 with my cost for copies $3.66/Standard and $2.15/Pro. After checking similar books on Amazon I enter a list price of $18.95. At $18.95, my Royalty through Amazon.com and affiliates will be $7.71/Standard and $9.22/Pro. Through the E-Store my Royalty is $11.50/Standard and $13.01/Pro.

Clicking Save Changes opens the Add Files page and red error messages, one that I need to edit the cover, and another that I haven't uploaded an interior file.

Upgrade your Publishing Plan!

Keep more of each sale of this book and pay less when you order copies by going Pro! Learn More

☆ **Pro** Plan **$39.00**

| Upgrade |

Your cost to order multiple copies:

| 📖 | Standard | **$14.23 each** |
| 📖 | Pro | **$8.13 each** |

See below for the royalty you earn for sales.

List Price

* **List Price**

how to set the price...

| 23.72 | | Update List Price |

Minimum publish-at price for this title is $23.72

As the author or publisher, you set the list price for your title. If your title has a list price above our publish-at rate, you are eligible for royalty payments on sales of that title. Sales of titles whose list price is at our publish-at rate will not earn royalty payments. We may decline publication of titles whose list price is below our publish-at rate. The publish-at rate may change based on the distribution channel(s) selected.

Amazon.com Retail Sales

Currently: Enabled | Disable |

Browse Keywords | Reference |

Amazon.com Retail Royalty Calculation

For more info see Content License Royalties

	Standard	☆ **Pro**	
List Price (set by you)	$23.72	$23.72	
Our Share	$23.72	$17.62	see more info on how we calculate our share
Your Royalty	**$0.00**	**$6.10**	list price minus our share

Note: Changes to your title, including list price, may take up to 15 business days to appear on Amazon.com.

E-Store Sales

Currently: Enabled | Disable |

E-Store Type | Public |

* **Sales Region** | US and international sales |

Only affects eStore sales

E-Store Royalty Calculation

For more info see Content License Royalties

	Standard	☆ **Pro**	
List Price (set by you)	$23.72	$23.72	
Our Share	$18.98	$12.88	see more info on how we calculate our share
Your Royalty	**$4.74**	**$10.84**	list price minus our share

Note: Discounts you set in your member account are considered reductions to your list price for the purpose of calculating your royalty.

To print this book in full color, the minimum list price must be $23.72 which nets me $0 royalties under the Standard Publishing Plan.

Upgrade your Publishing Plan!

Keep more of each sale of this book and pay less when you order copies by going Pro! Learn More

☆ **Pro** Plan **$39.00**   Upgrade

Your cost to order multiple copies:

Standard   **$14.23 each**

Pro   **$8.13 each**

See below for the royalty you earn for sales.

List Price

* **List Price**   29.95   Update List Price

how to set the price...   Minimum publish-at price for this title is $23.72

As the author or publisher, you set the list price for your title. If your title has a list price above our publish-at rate, you are eligible for royalty payments on sales of that title. Sales of titles whose list price is at our publish-at rate will not earn royalty payments. We may decline publication of titles whose list price is below our publish-at rate. The publish-at rate may change based on the distribution channel(s) selected.

Amazon.com Retail Sales

Currently: Enabled   Disable

Browse Keywords   Reference

Amazon.com Retail Royalty Calculation   For more info see Content License Royalties

	Standard	☆ Pro	
List Price (set by you)	$29.95	$29.95	
Our Share	$26.21	$20.11	see more info on how we calculate our share
Your Royalty	**$3.74**	**$9.84**	list price minus our share

Note: Changes to your title, including list price, may take up to 15 business days to appear on Amazon.com.

E-Store Sales

Currently: Enabled   Disable

E-Store Type   Public

* **Sales Region**   US and international sales

Only affects eStore sales

E-Store Royalty Calculation   For more info see Content License Royalties

	Standard	☆ Pro	
List Price (set by you)	$29.95	$29.95	
Our Share	$20.22	$14.12	see more info on how we calculate our share
Your Royalty	**$9.73**	**$15.83**	list price minus our share

Note: Discounts you set in your member account are considered reductions to your list price for the purpose of calculating your royalty.

In full color, with a list price of $29.95, my royalties under the Standard Plan are $3.74. The price has increased by $6.23 and Amazon's 40% increases proportionately.

Upgrade your Publishing Plan!

Keep more of each sale of this book and pay less when you order copies by going Pro! Learn More

☆ **Pro** Plan   **$39.00**   [Upgrade]

Your cost to order multiple copies:

Standard	$3.66 each
Pro	$2.15 each

See below for the royalty you earn for sales.

List Price

* List Price   18.95   [Update List Price]

how to set the price...   Minimum publish-at price for this title is $6.10

As the author or publisher, you set the list price for your title. If your title has a list price above our publish-at rate, you are eligible for royalty payments on sales of that title. Sales of titles whose list price is at our publish-at rate will not earn royalty payments. We may decline publication of titles whose list price is below our publish-at rate. The publish-at rate may change based on the distribution channel(s) selected.

Amazon.com Retail Sales

Currently: Enabled   [Disable]

Browse Keywords   Reference

Amazon.com Retail Royalty Calculation   For more info see Content License Royalties

	Standard	☆ Pro	
List Price (set by you)	$18.95	$18.95	
Our Share	$11.24	$9.73	see more info on how we calculate our share
Your Royalty	**$7.71**	**$9.22**	list price minus our share

Note: Changes to your title, including list price, may take up to 15 business days to appear on Amazon.com.

E-Store Sales

Currently: Enabled   [Disable]

E-Store Type   Public

* Sales Region   US and international sales

Only affects eStore sales

E-Store Royalty Calculation   For more info see Content License Royalties

	Standard	☆ Pro	
List Price (set by you)	$18.95	$18.95	
Our Share	$7.45	$5.94	see more info on how we calculate our share
Your Royalty	**$11.50**	**$13.01**	list price minus our share

Note: Discounts you set in your member account are considered reductions to your list price for the purpose of calculating your royalty.

Changing the interior to black & white and revising the list price to $18.95, my royalties under the Standard Plan are $7.71 and my cost for copies is $3.66.

I'm not ready to upload a file so I ignore the message. When my files are ready to submit, I will deal with any incomplete items in the setup.

Review Setup

At the Review Setup page, all the information I've completed so far is shown as well as the cover error messages.

When I click on Edit then Edit Cover on the next page, Cover Creator opens and my completed cover appears to be missing. When I click on The Oak template, my cover reappears, configured to fit the current page count and paper choice. I click Cover Complete - Save Changes, and once the new file is saved, the cover error messages disappear.

The Incomplete in the Add Files section will remain until I submit the PDF for the interior pages.

Title Information (Complete) Edit

Title ID	3405602
Title	How to be a Self-Published Author
Subtitle	A Step-by-Step Guide
Volume Number	1
Description	Self-publishing is not rocket science. Today's technology makes it simple for authors who are fairly computer savvy to also self publish. This guide, written by a publishing consultant and self-publis...
ISBN	0982561709
EAN-13	9780982561706
Imprint Name	Home & Leisure Publishing, Inc.
Primary Category	Reference / Writing Skills
Country of Publication	United States
Language	English
Search Keywords	publishing;how to publish a book;self-publisher;getting published
Contributors	*Authored by* Pat Gaudette

Physical Properties (Complete) Edit

Number of Pages	104
Interior Type	Black and White
Trim Size	8" x 10"
Binding	US Trade Paper
Paper Color	White

Add Files (Incomplete) Edit

Book Cover

Oct 18 2009

Sales Channel Management (Complete) Edit

Pro	No
List Price	$18.95
Sell via Amazon Retail Sales	Yes
Amazon Retail Sales status	Requested
Sell via E-Store Sales	Yes
Type of E-Store	Public
Sales Region	US and international sales

I used Cover Creator to design a book cover but in order to have text on the spine, I had to increase the page count from 104 to 134. I don't know if this is a problem with Cover Creator, CreateSpace, or both.

Lightning Source will print spine text on books with as few as 80 pages so I designed the cover again, using a Lightning Source cover template. I won't know until I submit the cover file if CreateSpace will accept it.

The last step is to upload the PDF of the text block and wait for email confirmation that my file meets CreateSpace's requirements to print. If it does, I'll receive another email advising that I can order a proof copy.

After reviewing the proof, I can either make changes to the cover and text files, resubmit them and order another proof, or approve the proof so the book is available for purchase on Amazon.com and their affiliated sites. Once approved, the book will also be available through my CreateSpace E-Store. After my files are submitted for printing, I will set up my E-Store and sign up for the Pro Plan.

The nice thing about using CreateSpace is that even after I have approved the book and it is available for sale, I can make changes to the cover and minor edits to the book block without incurring any charges except the cost of a new proof. The negative is that each time a revision is submitted, book sales will be put on hold until the new proof is approved.

Graphics

Image and graphic files in the book interior must be at 300 dpi or higher or CreateSpace's preflight (pre-print review) of the PDF will generate error messages that the quality of the images is poor. The error messages can be ignored but the images may not print as well as expected. As an example, here is a photograph from *Sparky the AIBO* saved in 100, 200, and 300 dpi resolutions.

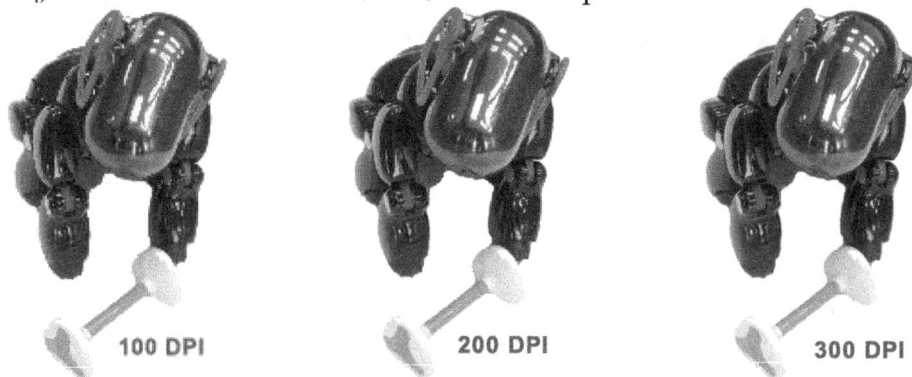

100 DPI   **200 DPI**   **300 DPI**

CreateSpace Distribution

Once this book is uploaded, and the proof is ordered and approved, it will be listed and available for purchase on Amazon.com and Amazon's affiliate sites. That information is shown in Sales Channel Management which is part of Print Ready/ Purchase Ready in the CreateSpace control panel.

Just below Sales Channel Management is an edit link for the book's CreateSpace E-Store which must be set up once the book is available for purchase. The E-Store link can be added to webpages or emails and E-Store purchases will generate a higher royalty than sales on Amazon.com. The screenshot to the left is the information for *Teen Mom*.

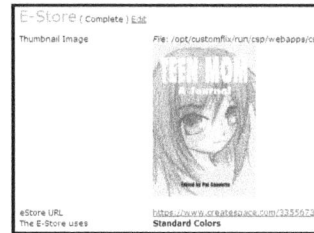

It would be a benefit if items in CreateSpace E-Stores were searchable or listed in an open area of CreateSpace but, when I tried to find my E-Stores and books on the CreateSpace website, I couldn't.

The Merger of CreateSpace and BookSurge

As this book goes to press, this announcement is on the CreateSpace site:

> *CreateSpace will soon become the dedicated publishing and print on-demand platform for all BookSurge and CreateSpace authors and publishers. BookSurge and CreateSpace have historically operated as two distinct brands of one company—On-Demand Publishing LLC, a subsidiary of Amazon.com, Inc.—and are now uniting on the CreateSpace platform and brand.*

> *During the coming months, we will be transitioning all BookSurge accounts to CreateSpace, after which the BookSurge brand will be retired. In addition, BookSurge's publishing services are now available on the CreateSpace platform, enabling CreateSpace members to benefit from the same knowledgeable staff that has supported BookSurge members for years.*

Lightning Source
www.LightningSource.com

Now that you have used CreateSpace to publish your book, you can set up an account with Lightning Source to take advantage of their print-on-demand service both in the U.S. and overseas, and to get your book into their huge distribution network.

Lightning Source is a printer, not a publisher. They work with publishers, the biggest and the smallest. They provide print-on-demand and offset printing services, and they are the largest print-on-demand printer in the U.S. When a subsidiary publisher touts book distribution through Ingram, Baker & Taylor, etc., you can be sure they are using Lightning Source's services.

There is no cost to set up an account with Lightning Source. The costs will come from the services requested as well as the normal costs of being in the publishing business, even as a one-person publishing house.

Lightning Source Services
Print to Order (or Print on Demand) is the service LSI is most known for and the one I use. I set the retail price of my books, the wholesale discount, and the return policy (I don't accept returns). Lightning Source provides my book information to their distribution partners (including Ingram, Baker & Taylor, Barnes & Noble, and Amazon.com).

Distributors receive orders for books from wholesalers and retailers, and submit the orders to Lightning Source. Lightning Source prints orders when received (on demand), ships, collects the wholesale price, deducts their print charge, and pays the balance to me. The Print to Order fee is $12 per year per title.

Print to Publisher: Lightning Source receives orders from publishers, prints the quantities specified, from one to 5000+, and ships to consumers, retailers, and/or warehouses using the publisher's logo so that it appears the order has come directly from the publisher. Lightning Source charges for printing, handling, and shipping. Smaller quantities are printed digitally, offset printing is offered on paperback quantities over 2,000 and hardcover quantities over 750.

Print to Warehouse: Lightning Source prints and ships quantities to publisher's warehouse. They charge for printing, handling, and shipping. This option is primarily designed for large publishing houses.

Digital Print Runs: Publishers needing to keep a small inventory for their own use get a volume discount on quantities of 25 or more of a single title delivered to one location.

Offset Press Runs: When quantities are high, offset printing can be the most cost effective print method. Lightning Source offers offset printing for minimum orders of 1500 paperback or 750 hardcover copies of a title.

ISBN Publisher Prefix

To use Lightning Source for printing your book, as you would an offset printer, you don't need an ISBN account number. However, you must have an ISBN for your book to be printed through LSI's Print to Order (POD) service and to get into LSI's distribution network.

All distributors, wholesalers, and retailers require an ISBN on every book they handle. The ISBN, or International Standard Book Number, identifies the title and publisher of a book and allows booksellers a way to accurately order books.

Each ISBN is used only once and each version of a book (hardcover, softcover, ebook, revision, audio book, etc.) must have a separate ISBN. The ISBN number is included on the copyright page and a bar code including ISBN is printed on the outside back cover.

If you're a resident or business in the United States, go to www.isbn.org to complete the online application through R.R. Bowker, the U.S. ISBN Agency. If you are not in the United States, the site has links and information about the designated ISBN agents for other countries.

I have had a few calls from major bookstores asking that I ship one or two books to them because they looked up the publisher information for the ISBN on the particular book they want. Rather than get involved in direct distribution, I ask them to place the order through Ingram Book Company, usually their regular book distributor.

Pay specific attention to the cautions on the ISBN website regarding purchase of ISBNs from sellers other than R.R. Bowker. ISBNs are usually sold in blocks of 10 or more but Bowker now sells a single ISBN for $125 or a single ISBN plus bar code for $150.

If you don't expect to ever publish another book or another version of your current book, then the $125 or $150 deal might be right for you. Otherwise, opt for the block of 10 for $325. (Prices as of November 2009.)

I planned to use an ISBN from the original block of ten purchased when I began self-publishing but all ten are already in use. The new block of ISBNs has a different Publisher Prefix since each "block" cannot be added onto at a later date.

LCCN and PCN Numbers

Now that you have your ISBN(s), you'll want to apply for a Preassigned Control Number from the Library of Congress in order to include the applicable Library of Congress Control Number (LCCN) on your copyright page.

Go to the website at http://pcn.loc.gov and click on "Scope" to make sure that your book will qualify for the program. If it does, click on "Open New Account" and complete the "Application to Participate" in the PCN Program.

Once approved, log in and complete a Preassigned Control Number Application for your book. Unlike ISBNs, separate LCCNs are not required for different versions of the same book. There is no cost other than sending a copy of your published book to the Library of Congress.

Required information in the PCN Application, marked by asterisks, includes Title, Publisher, U.S. City and State, approximate number of pages, projected publication date, and your contact information. Include your complete name in the "Enter the fullest form of the first author's name" blocks. Then type your name as you'll use it on your title page in the next block.

As soon as you complete and submit the PCN Application you'll receive an email acknowledging receipt. Depending upon the current volume of applications, it may take a week or more before you receive the LCCN. I received the LCCN for this book the day after I submitted the application.

The LCCN information must be displayed on your copyright page as: "Library of Congress Control Number: 2009909981." (That is my LCCN for this book.)

If you are assigned an LCCN for your book, you *must* send a copy of the published book, as soon as it is published, to the Library of Congress for their files or risk being suspended from the program.

Completing The Lightning Source Application

By setting up a Lightning Source account and buying one or more ISBNs, you keep control of your book and the current and future profits. If a major publishing house shows interest after you have published it, negotiations will be between you and the interested publisher.

To set up a new account with Lightning Source you will have to complete the online application at www.LightningSource.com. Once you've completed the application, you will be provided with a checklist and one or more PDF documents to download, print, complete, and sign. Documents may include resale tax certificates, W9 forms, and POD contract(s).

When you have faxed or mailed the required contracts and forms, and Lightning Source has received and reviewed the required information, your account will be activated, and you may begin submitting titles and placing orders through the LSI website.

When your application is accepted, go to "Login" at the very top of the Lightning Source homepage and log in to your account. Take time to look through the various sections of your control panel, and, when you're ready to set up a book, go to My Account > Operating Manuals & Contract Documents.

Before Lightning Source will print or distribute your books they must receive a signed copy of the US POD Agreement if your company is in the United States. The POD Agreement is in Adobe PDF format. This may have been a required document during the applicaton process; if not, download, print, complete, and sign a copy now. Fax or mail it to Lightning Source. If you're in the US and would also like UK POD printing and distribution, you'll need to print, sign, and mail or fax the UK POD Agreement. Contracts and Agreements you have signed with Lightning Source will be listed in your control panel.

Download and print a copy of the POD Operating Manual (US or UK) for everything you'll need to know including book sizes, types (softcover, hardcover, case laminate, glassbook), file requirements, the cost to submit files for printing, and the cost to order books. The print cost is a fixed price as indicated in the POD Operating Manual.

Submitting a Book to Lightning Source

Log into your LSI account and then click on My Library and choose Setup a New Title Setup from the dropdown box. For current step-by-step instructions in PDF format, click on the *Setting up a New Title* link on the page.

New Title Setup: I select Title for Full Distribution Services – (includes Wholesale US/UK/EU Distribution and Publisher Direct Distribution) and leave the checkboxes for eBook unchecked. I can do the preliminary setup for this book even though it is not ready to submit because I am setting up the print version. If I later publish it as an eBook, I will have to do a new setup when the files are ready for upload.

Lightning Source™

Welcome, Home & Leisure Publishing, Inc | Request Assistance | Account at a Glance

My Account | My Library | My Orders | Logout   FAQs

New Title Setup

You can learn more about **Setting up a New Title**, or select the desired title setup option, then select ""Continue"".

Print On Demand Set Up Options:

    ⊙ Title for Full Distribution Services - (includes Wholesale US/UK/EU Distribution and Publisher Direct Distribution)

    ○ Title for Publisher Direct Distribution - Short Run Only

eBook Set Up Options:

  Only select eBook formats for which you have files ready to upload now

    Microsoft Reader

    Adobe eBook

    Palm Reader

Title General Information: My Publisher Name and Number is already filled in. If I was using an imprint for this book, which I'm not, it would go into the Imprint block.

- Pub. Ref. Number is an optional field and I'm leaving it blank.
- ISBN: 0-9825617-0-9 (dashes must be included)
- Title: How To Be A Self-Published Author: A Step-by-Step Guide
- Language: English
- Subject 1: Computers: Digital Media - Desktop Publishing
- Subject 2: Computers: Electronic Publishing
- Subject 3: Language Arts & Disciplines: Publishing
- Contributors: 1: Gaudette, Pat - Author

Title General Information

Publisher:	**Home & Leisure Publishing, Inc**	
Publisher Number:	**6024978**	
? Imprint:	Home & Leisure Publishing, Inc	
? Pub. Ref. Number:		
? ISBN:	0-9825617-0-9	Autofill Title Metadata
? Title:	How To Be A Self-Published Author: A Step-by-Step Guide	
? Language:	English	

? Subjects:

Subject 1:	Computers : Digital Media - Desktop Publishing	Find subjects
Subject 2:	Computers : Electronic Publishing	Find subjects
Subject 3:	Language Arts & Disciplines : Publishing	Find subjects

Contributors:

Last Name	First	Middle	Role
1. Gaudette	Pat		Author

Print On Demand General Information: There are some required items that I am unable to complete since this book is not ready to submit.

- Ingram Adv. Catalog? Selecting Yes shows the fees for the US, UK and EU (these are all of my signed agreements).
- Content Type: B&W
- Paper Type: White
- Binding: B&W 8 x 10 in or 254 x 203 mm Perfect Bound on White
- Publication Date: 11-13-2009.
- Page Count: 104
- Market Pricing: I decide on a US List Price of $18.95, a 55% Discount, and "No" the books are not returnable. I will complete the UK pricing later.
- Book Description: This wording is important marketing text. It must get the interest of booksellers and it is what they may use when they list it for sale.

Print On Demand General Information

√   ? Ingram Adv. Catalog?   [Yes (Fees: US $60/UK £40/EU €50) ▼]   Ingram Advance Fees

NOTE:
Lightning Source offers the following trim sizes for books with Black & White (B&W) or Color interiors.
Some of these trim sizes are available on either White or Crème paper. Please select your binding type carefully.

Content Type: ⦿ B&W ○ Color

Paper Type: ○ Creme ⦿ White

√   ? Binding: [B&W 8.000 x 10.000 in or 254 x 203mm Perfect Bound on White   ▼]

	Left Justified	Center	Right Justified
? Cloth Spine Text:	[ ]	[ ]	[ ]

√   ? Publication Date: [11/13/2009] ▦ (mm/dd/yyyy)

√   ? Page Count: [104]

Market Pricing:

▸ ? Market	◂ ? List Price	◂ ? Discount	▸ ? Returnable?
☑ United States	[18.95] USD	[55] %	[No ▼]
☐ United Kingdom	[0.00] GBP	[0] %	[▼]
☐ Canada	[0.00] CAD	[0] %	[▼]
☐ European Union	[0.00] EUR	[0] %	[▼]
☐ Australia	[0.00] AUD	[0] %	[▼]

? Book Description (formally called "Annotation")
NOTE:
This is text describing your book, used by booksellers to describe and market your book on their websites. This is not set-up instructions.

Self-publishing is not rocket science and current technology enables computer-savvy authors to also be self-published. This step-by-step guide, written by a publishing consultant and self-published author, is for authors who are tired of waiting for someone else to publish their books.

Print On Demand Content: This is where I let Lightning Source know what type of materials I will supply and the method (File Upload, CD, Jaz or Zip, Hard Copy). Costs vary depending upon the method; specifications for each and the costs are listed in the POD Operating Manual.

- Cover - File Upload
- Interior - File Upload
- Will you be placing an order for a proof after you submit your file? Yes
- Special Instructions: These are instructions for the product and press people. I write that my cover and interior pages are Full Bleed so that I don't get messages about my text or images being outside the trim space.
- Promotion Code: Blank
- Large Text Format: Unchecked
- Espresso: Checked

Print On Demand Content

Supplying	Content Type	Media	? Return Materials (at publisher's expense)
☑	Cover	File Upload	☑
☑	Interior	File Upload	☑

? **Will you be placing an order for a proof after you submit your title?** [Yes(Fee)]

? **Special Instructions:**

Special title processing instructions only. Please do not include comments for Client Services, i.e., "Please expedite this title". Comments for Client Services should be emailed to your Client Services Representative.

Other Title Information:

Promotion Code : [   ]

Large Text Edition : ☑

Espresso : ☑

Saving this page, I'm at the Titles Not Yet Submitted (Work In Progress) page which now includes the listing for this book. The What next? dropdown box to the right of the listing defaults to Nothing Now; other options are Submit and Delete. Delete will completely remove the title information from my account; Submit means I'm ready to upload my cover and interior files.

Lightning Source™

Titles Not Yet Submitted (Work In Progress)

Sort by: ISBN

= Ready to Submit

ISBN	Title	Contributor	Last Modified	What next?
0982561709	How To Be A Self-Published Author: A Step-by-Step Guide	Gaudette, Pat	10/21/2009 10:53:58 AM	Nothing Now

To make changes to the listing, I click the title and can now change anything I need to, clicking Save to move from page to page. Until this book is submitted and ready for orders, it won't appear on my Current Titles page.

ISBN/SKU	Binding	Title	Contributor	Submit Date	Status
9780976121084	Perfect	Teen Mom: A Journal	Gaudette, Pat	4/14/2009	Available for Printing/Download
9780976121091	Trade Cloth	Teen Mom: A Journal	Gaudette, Pat	1/13/2009	Available for Printing/Download
9780976121060	Trade Cloth	Sparky the AIBO: Robot Dogs & Other Robotic Pets	Gaudette, Pat	3/1/2005	Available for Printing/Download
0976121050	Glassbook	Midnight Confessions: True Stories of Adultery	Gaudette, Pat	12/30/2004	Available for Printing/Download
0976121042	Perfect	Midnight Confessions: True Stories of Adultery	Gaudette, Pat	12/20/2004	Available for Printing/Download
0976121034	Glassbook	Advice for an Imperfect Married World	Gaudette, Pat	10/19/2004	Available for Printing/Download
0976121026	Perfect	Advice for an Imperfect Married World	Gaudette, Pat	10/19/2004	Available for Printing/Download
0976121018	Glassbook	Advice for an Imperfect Single World: Wisdom and Wit from Friends & Lovers' Queen of Hearts	Gaudette, Pat	9/10/2004	Available for Printing/Download
097612100X	Perfect	Advice for an Imperfect Single World: Wisdom and Wit from Friends & Lovers' Queen of Hearts	Gaudette, Pat	9/9/2004	Available for Printing/Download

Cover Generator

To create a cover template, I log out of my account and return to the Lightning Source home page, click on File Creation, and then select Cover Template Generator from the dropdown box. The Lightning Source Cover Generator is not the same as CreateSpace's Cover Creator. It is a blank template showing trim lines, safe areas for images and text, and proper placement of the bar code on the back cover.

The template can be generated in several formats: InDesign, QuarkExpress, PDF or EPS. The template file is emailed to the publisher and can then be provided to the graphic artist doing the cover design.

Because I have already set this book up in my LSI account, the book details are automatically filled in once I type the ISBN in the first block.

The List Price does not have to be included on the bar code. I choose not to include it in case I want to change the price in the future. If the price was included it would show up as 51895 but the null code of 90000 will be printed instead.

Lightning Source Cover Generator

Once you complete and submit the form below, LSI will email you back a template and support files to be used to build your cover. Included in the email will be instructions for using the template, creating an appropriate PostScript file and distilling a PDF to LSI specifications.

√ Required Fields

√ **ISBN (with dashes):**	0-9825617-0-9 (10 digit ISBN entries will be converted to the correct 13 digit ISBN number)
?**Publisher Reference Number:**	
Content Type:	⦿ B&W ○ Color
Paper Type:	○ Creme ⦿ White
√ **Book Type:**	B&W 8.000 x 10.000 in or 254 x 203mm Perfect Bound on White
√ **Page Count:**	104 (Multiple of 2, between 48 and 828)
√ **File Type to Return:**	EPS
√ **Email Address:**	Info@halpi.com
√ **Retype Email Address:**	info@halpi.com

Optional Information:

Price (including decimal):	18.95	**Currency:**	US Dollars
Price in Bar Code:	No		

The Cost To Make This Book POD Ready

Ingram Advance Catalog: $60.00 for U.S. publishers. Ingram Advance is a monthly print catalog distributed by Ingram Book Group to booksellers and libraries around the world. This one-time marketing service is available to publishers only at the time they submit a title to Lightning Source for initial setup.

The listing in the print catalog appears three or four months after a title has been approved to print at Lightning Source. The listing includes a black & white image of the book's front cover, a short paragraph about the book (the Book Description wording), and retail pricing details.

Digital Catalog Fee: $12 at setup and annually thereafter. According to the LSI website, this fee includes: Standardized BISAC subject coding with up to 3 subject categories (I chose the categories during book setup); Detailed title listing in all daily catalogs LSI provides to its US and International distribution partners; Title summary inclusion in LSI's enhanced bibliographic catalog feed; Storage and backup of both title content and bibliographic data; Price and discount maintenance for publisher price changes.

Cover File Upload: $37.50 per cover file; each version of a book (paperback, hardcover, case laminate) is an additional $37.50. While each version of a title might have the same cover design, the bar code on the back will change. Each revision is a new charge.

Interior File Upload: $37.50 per text file. As with the cover, each version of the text file will incur an additional $37.50 charge as will each revision.

Proof: $30.00 (includes overnight shipping).

TOTAL: $177.00.

The $177.00 total does not include the cost for the ISBN(s), revisions once the proof is reviewed, and any payments made to graphic artists, editors, or anyone else hired to get the book ready to print.

I cut the cost of revisions by first publishing through CreateSpace. Once I'm satisfied with the printed book through CreateSpace, I submit the files to Lightning Source.

Profit To Self-Publisher Per Book Sold

Lightning Source emails a monthly statement to publishers showing the number of books sold, retail price, discount, their print cost, and the net to the publisher. They can either mail paper checks or do direct bank deposits when monies are payable.

The current price to print an 8x10 paperback book through LSI is $3.24 per unit for books 48-104 pages in size. Over 104 pages the cost would be $1.30 per unit plus $.018 per page. This book is 104 pages in size so the print cost will be $3.24.

Retail Price ($18.95) - 55% Discount ($10.42) = $8.53 - Print Cost ($3.24) = $5.29 Net to Publisher per POD book ordered through Lightning Source.

As the Author/Publisher, the $5.29 equates to my "royalty" per book sold. I will have to sell quite a few copies in order to recoup my set up costs and other expenses.

Benefit of POD Printing Through Lightning Source

Once a book has been submitted and approved for printing, it becomes a part of the most comprehensive book distribution network in the world. It is the publisher's choice whether to make the book available for distribution within the U.S. only or to the U.K. and European markets.

During title setup, I checked the "Espresso" block on the Print On Demand Content Page. By doing this, the book will also be available for purchase through the Espresso Book Machine, a print on demand machine that is targeted to retail bookstores and libraries.

The Espresso Book Machine (EBM) prints, collates, covers, and binds a single paperback book in just minutes. Bookstores with the EBM no longer must stock a huge, and expensive, assortment of books in order to meet the needs of a wide range of buyers. The EBM has access to the files of millions of books, both current and out of print. To watch an EBM in action, visit YouTube.com and search for "Espresso Book Machine."

The same PDF cover and text files submitted to Lightning Source for their POD services are used to print the book through the Espresso Book Machine. With EBMs being placed in locations throughout the world, the distribution potential is virtually unlimited.

eBook
Publishing

Ebooks have been sold as downloadable PDFs for years and there's no reason a book can't be published, sold, and distributed in PDF format. I have several "glassbooks" distributed through Lightning Source, which also were also being sold through Amazon.com until Amazon introduced the Kindle and stopped selling all ebooks except those formatted for the Kindle.

Unfortunately, not all books are good candidates for the Kindle. Books that are dependent on graphics and fancy layouts won't fare well when they are reformatted to the Kindle's "reflowable" format, designed to be displayed on screens of varying sizes both in width and height. Add in the reader's choice as to text size and it's very difficult to predict how a complex page will look.

I set up three Kindle books in 2008: *Advice for an Imperfect Single World*, *Advice for an Imperfect Married World*, and *Midnight Confessions*. I did not set up a Kindle version of *Sparky the AIBO* because of the number of photographs throughout the book. Since I had not published a Kindle version of *Teen Mom*, I decided to publish it while writing this section.

To publish using Amazon's Digital Text Platform, sign up at http://dtp.amazon.com or, if you already have an Amazon.com account, sign in on the same page. To create an Amazon account you'll need to provide your name, a valid email address, and a password.

Next, you'll need to set up your DTP account. An ISBN is not required to publish a book through DTP. What is required is a US bank account and a valid Social Security Number, Tax ID Number, or Employer ID Number. Lastly, you'll have to agree to comply with the Digital Text Platform Terms and Conditions. This is a legal contract so take time to make sure you understand what you're agreeing to and if you have questions, this is the time to consult with an attorney.

The Terms and Conditions include wording that allows for future distribution through other devices. As of November 2009, Kindle books can be downloaded to the Amazon Kindle, the iPhone, the iPod touch, and they can be read on a computer by downloading Amazon's free Kindle for PC software (Windows 7, Vista, and XP). The Mac version of the software should be available by the time this book is published.

The DTP publisher pages are not complex. There are five choices at the top of each page: My Shelf, My Reports, My Account, Help, and Sign Out.

The "My Account" page has company name, address, business type, EIN, and bank information.

The "My Reports" page has options to view reports for the current month, previous months, and year to date, all in Excel spreadsheet format.

The "My Shelf" page contains information about books published and it is where new books are added. My "My Shelf" lists the three eBooks I published in 2008.

There are three steps to publishing on the Digital Text Platform:

1) Enter Product Details;

2) Upload & Preview Book;

3) Enter Price.

Product Details

I completed the Product Details, including choosing five categories for *Teen Mom* to be listed in. I was unsuccessful in uploading a cover file because, even though the box for uploading an image did allow me to browse and find the file on my computer, there was no "Upload" button once I found the file.

Upload & Preview Book

This step was the most time-consuming. The DTP accepts content in several forms: HTML (.html, .htm), Zipped HTML for content containing images or multiple files (.zip), Mobipocket (.mobi, .prc), Microsoft Word (.doc), Plain Text (.txt), and Adobe PDF (.pdf).

DTP first converts uploaded files into HTML so the preferred format to upload is HTML. To convert a Word .doc or .txt file into HTML, open the file in Microsoft Word then from the File menu choose Save As, and in the Save As Type dropdown box, choose Web Page. Once the file is saved as .html or .htm, the file can be opened and viewed in a web browser to check for errors. If there are problems, they can be corrected by editing the HTML code.

The only file available for upload for *Teen Mom* was the PDF file exported from Pagemaker. Even though I started out with some plain text files, they were imported into Pagemaker and the bulk of the editing and writing took place simultaneously with the typography and page layout. I knew from experience that the conversion from PDF to HTML would be tedious and ugly.

In April of 2008, in order to sell eBooks through Amazon.com, it was necessary to sign up for a publisher account with Mobipocket (www.mobipocket.com). The lines blurred between Amazon and Mobipocket with emails from "Amazon Digital

Text" providing Kindle Publishing Guidelines and Updates, and emails from Mobipocket containing quarterly eBookbase Statements.

One of the first emails I received from Amazon after signing up with Mobipocket included this statement: "Mobipocket's eBookBase will continue to serve as the single location for you to manage your eBook submissions, information, and pricing for the Mobipocket.com, Amazon.com, and eBookBase member retailer websites."

Even though Mobipocket's file format is, according to their website, "cross-platform and handle 100% of PDA/Smartphone market, which is the reference platcform for ebooks and also the PC and Tablet PC," I found the conversion process somewhat confusing.

Mobipocket is now owned by Amazon and this message appears on the Publishers login page: *"Effective September 2009, we will no longer open new accounts for publishers to sell titles through the Kindle Store or MobiPocket.com. If you have an existing account, there will be no change and you can continue to upload and sell titles using Ebookbase. New publishers with a US address and bank account can sign up to sell ebooks in the Kindle store via our self-service publishing channel at http://dtp.amazon.com."*

I mention this because one of the files that DTP accepts is the .prc file created by Mobipocket Creator, a free, downloadable program available at http://www.mobipocket.com/en/DownloadSoft/ProductDetailsCreator.asp. The software has many functions but the one that I needed was the PDF to HTML converter. The

Teen Mom PDF file had few embedded images, none which I considered important, and I wanted to see how well the PDF would convert to HTML.

I downloaded, installed, and opened the latest version of Mobipocket Creator. The home page of Creator has several options including

Create New Publication, Open Recent Publication, and Import From Existing File. I
clicked Adobe PDF from
the list under Import From
Existing File. This opened
up the Import File Wizard.

Next, I browsed my
computer to find the PDF
file to upload, created a
new folder for the
publication's files to be saved to, left English as the language, Encoding as Western,

then clicked the Import
button. After a few
seconds, a new window
opened and the publication
file for *Teen Mom* was listed
in .html format.

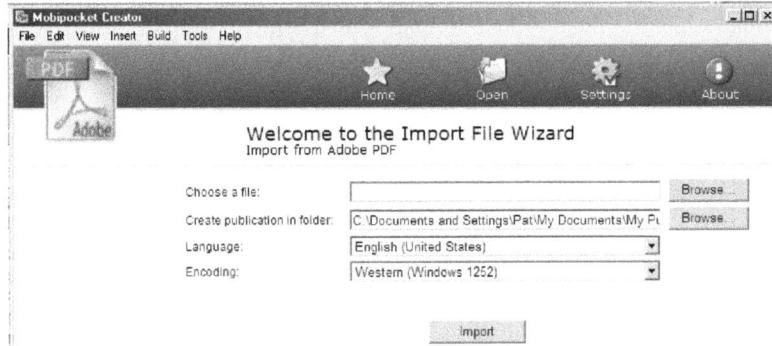

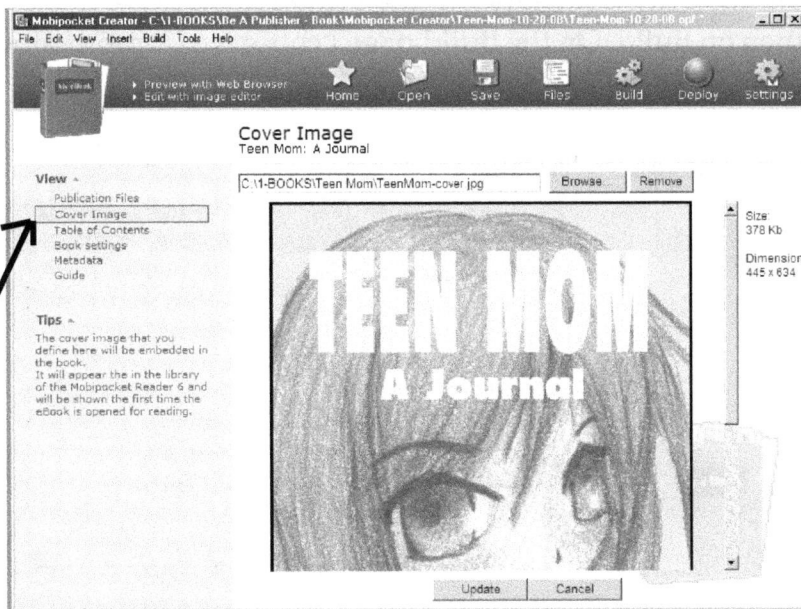

I clicked on Cover Image in the left column, uploaded a cover .jpg, and clicked
Update.

I then clicked on Book Settings and left the Encoding as Western, changed the Book Type to eBook, and clicked Update.

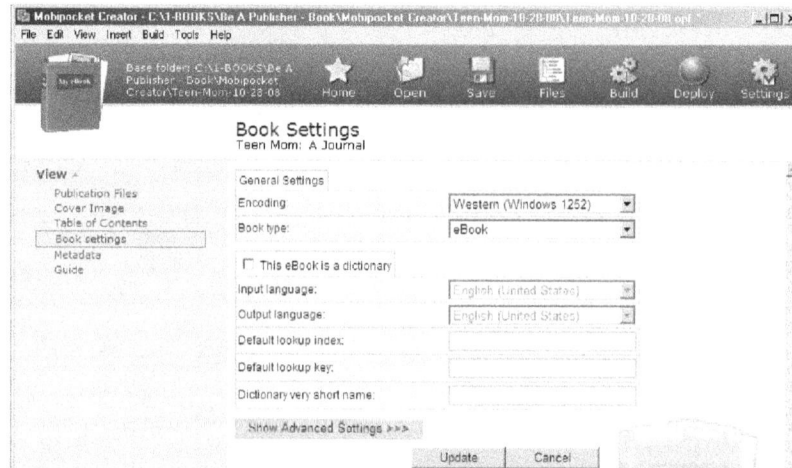

The Metadata window requires quite a bit of information (see opposite page): eBook Title, Author, Publisher, ISBN, Language, Main Subject, Description, review, Publishing Date, whether the book is Adult Only, Suggested Retail Price, and Territory Restriction (if any). Information that is necessary is marked with a red asterisk.

Once I completed the Metadata information, I clicked on the Save icon at the top of the page, then on Build. On the Build page I chose No Compression and Content Encryption with DRM (Digital Rights Management).

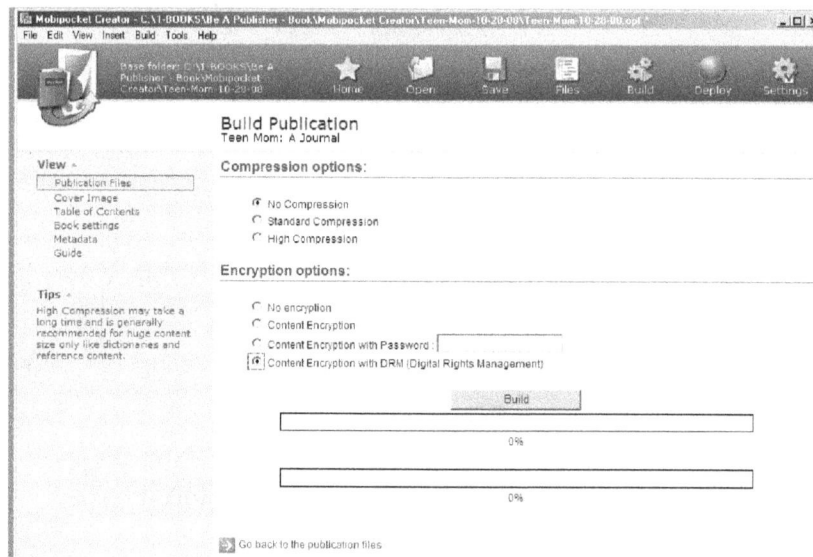

Mobipocket Creator - C:\1-BOOKS\Teen Mom\Teen_Mom_A_Journal\Teen_Mom_A_Journal\Teen_Mom_A_Journal.opf *

File Edit View Insert Build Tools Help

Base folder: C:\1-BOOKS\Teen Mom\Teen_Mom_A_Journal\Teen_Mom_A_Journal

Home | Open | Save | Files | Build | Deploy | Settings

Metadata
Teen Mom: A Journal

View
- Publication Files
- Cover Image
- Table of Contents
- Book settings
- Metadata
- Guide

Tips
Fields marked with a red star * are mandatory to deploy the eBook to wholesale distribution systems.

Metadata	Value	Information about this metadata
Mobipocket eBookBase ID:	241561	This book was already deployed. If you deploy it again, it will be updated.
eBook Title: *	Teen Mom: A Journal	150 characters maximum.
Author:	Gaudette, Pat	Last name comma first name (e.g. King, Stephen) Separate by semicolons (;) if more than one author.
Publisher:	Home & Leisure Publishing, Inc.	This information is embedded in the book but ignored by retailers; your publisher login determines the publisher information for this book on the retail websites.
ISBN:	978-0-9825617-1-3	Leave empty if you do not have an ISBN. If you have both a paper book ISBN and an eBook ISBN, use the eBook ISBN.
Language: *	English (United States)	
Main subject: *	Family	Your book will appear in this subject category on retailers websites

B *I* U | ≡ ≡ ≡ ≡ | <>

Description:

(4000 characters maximum)

Sixteen-year-old "Katie" was half way through her junior year of high school when she became pregnant. Throughout her pregnancy and for several months afterward, she kept a journal. This is her story as told in that journal.

Katie is not one teenager dealing with unplanned pregnancy, she is one of many. She may be the girl next door or the girl in the next block. She may be your daughter. She may be you.

Teens are more openly sexually active than in past generations and unplanned pregnancy is not the social stigma of years ago. The pregnancy of pop idol Britney Spears' 16-year-old

Review:

B *I* U | ≡ ≡ ≡ ≡ | <>

(2000 characters maximum)

| Publishing Date: | 11/13/2009 | You can leave this field empty to use the deploy date as publishing date. mm/dd/yyyy If set in the future, the book will not be available for sale on retail sites before this date. |
| Adult only: | ☐ | |

The cover image that you define here in the metadata will appear as cover art on retail websites. By default, this cover is the same as the cover image that you embed in the book but you can select a different image.

TeenMom-cover.jpg | Browse... | Use embedded cover

Cover image:

Demo PRC file:		Browse...	Leave empty unless you want a very specific demo book. If empty, a demo book will be generated automatically with the first 5% of the book.
Suggested Retail Price: *	11.95	US Dollars	
Territory Restriction:		Leave empty unless this book cannot be distributed worldwide.

Update | Cancel

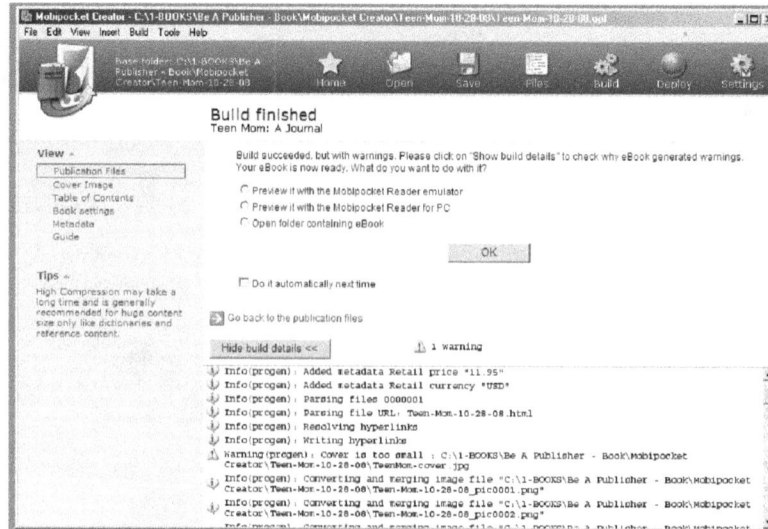

The Build Finished page indicates if the Build was successful and if not, what errors occurred. The first cover file I uploaded was over 150KB in size which caused Mobipocket Creator to arbitrarily reduce the file size to 50KB producing an error message that the file was too small during the Build. In Photoshop, I changed the cover file to 525 pixels wide by 700 pixels high and 147KB in size, uploaded the file, and clicked Build again. This time there was no error message.

At the Build Finished window are three options: Preview the eBook with the Mobipocket Reader emulator, Preview it with the Mobipocket Reader for PC, or Open folder containing eBook. I chose to see the files which had been created and clicked on the .html file.

Name	Size	Type	Date Modified
Teen-Mom-10-28-08.html	589 KB	HTML Document	11/15/2009 5:43 PM
Teen-Mom-10-28-08.opf	1 KB	OPF File	11/15/2009 6:09 PM
Teen-Mom-10-28-08.prc	845 KB	PRC File	11/15/2009 6:09 PM
Teen-Mom-10-28-08.xml	1,221 KB	XML Document	11/15/2009 5:43 PM
Teen-Mom-10-28-08_pic0001.png	582 KB	PNG File	11/15/2009 5:43 PM
Teen-Mom-10-28-08_pic0002.png	319 KB	PNG File	11/15/2009 5:43 PM
Teen-Mom-10-28-08_pic0003.png	354 KB	PNG File	11/15/2009 5:43 PM
Teen-Mom-10-28-08_pic0004.png	399 KB	PNG File	11/15/2009 5:43 PM
TeenMom-cover.jpg	50 KB	JPG File	11/15/2009 5:51 PM

It is important that the converted HTML file retain necessary page breaks and other formatting. When I looked at the HTML file in my web browser, more than 50% of the text had breaks between words that distorted the flow of the text. Much of the glossary and other back matter didn't have any breaks at all; the text was one mass of words. My only option was to edit the HTML file to remove incorrect coding, delete unnecessary graphics, and put in paragraph and page breaks. Once that was done, I opened Mobipocket Creator, deleted the PDF file, uploaded the corrected HTML file, clicked Build, and a new set of publication files was created.

Now that I had properly formatted Mobipocket files, specifically, the .prc file, I returned to my Amazon DTP account. At the Upload & Preview Book page I uploaded the Mobipocket .prc file and received a message that the upload was successful. The file was ready for preview.

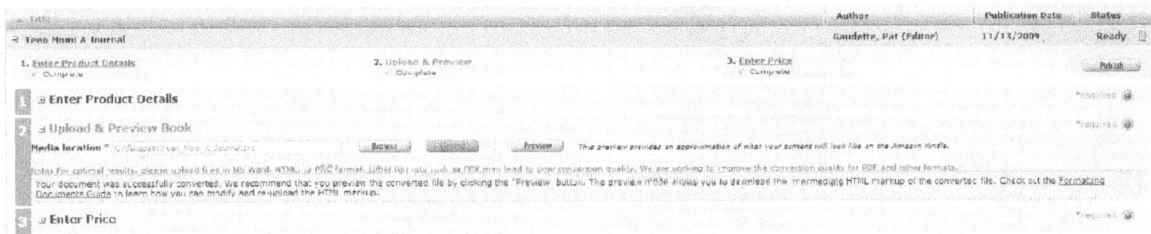

Clicking on the preview button shows how the book would appear on a Kindle.

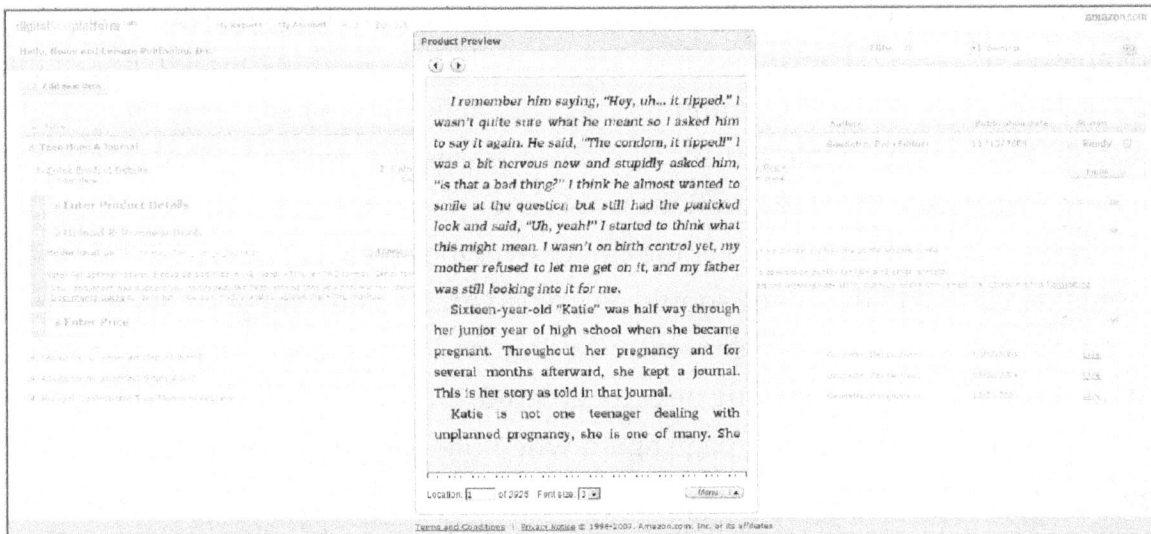

At the Enter Price page I type $11.95 and then click Publish.

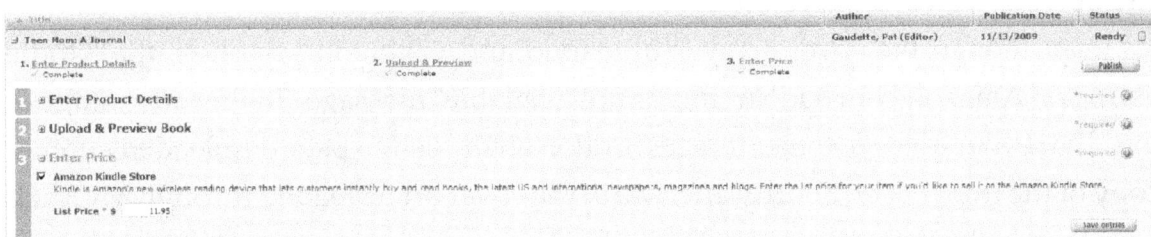

Previously my books were published immediately but this time this message appeared in "My Shelf." instead of the listing for *Teen Mom*:

"Publishing Teen Mom: A Journal. Your book is currently under review by the Kindle Operations team as we are trying to improve the Kindle customer experience. Please check back in 5 business days to see if your book was published to the store. This will not affect any titles you are currently selling in the store, but uploading updates to existing titles will take longer to process."

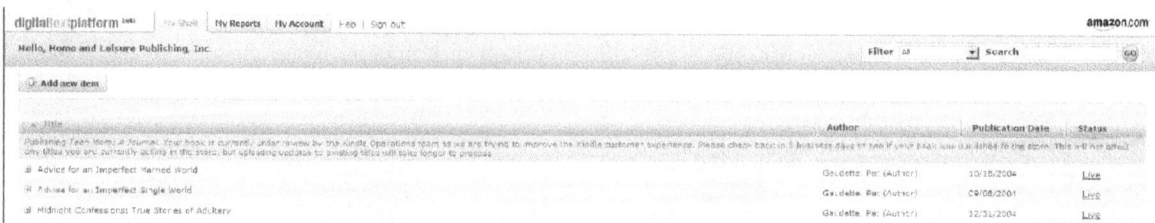

At this point I still haven't been able to upload a cover image to DTP and I look for answers on the DTP forums which are accessible by clicking the Help link at the top of the page. In the "Ask Community" section of the Forums, someone has already posted about being unable to upload a cover image due to the lack of an upload button. There were three suggestions from other posters.

The first suggestion is to hover the cursor over the area where the word "submit" should be, click, and the image should be uploaded. A second suggestion is to log in using Mozilla's Firefox browser since the button is visible in Firefox. The third suggestion is to save everything already entered, click on the Compatability View button, then open the upload page again when the page refreshes and the button should be visible.

Two days later the status of *Teen Mom* is shown as "Live" and I attempt to add a cover file. Mousing over the area where I think the button should be is unsuccessful so I open Firefox and successfully upload the cover art.

Even though the cover art was uploaded and visible in My Shelf, the Kindle listing on Amazon.com had an "image not available" message. Taking advantage of the "Share your own customer images" option on the listing page, I uploaded another copy of the front cover. Shortly afterward, the cover art uploaded through My Shelf appeared in the listing.

After publishing *Teen Mom* through the Digital Text Platform, I logged into my publisher account with Mobipocket and activated the copy of *Teen Mom* now listed in my eBook Catalog so that information about the book will be deployed to Mobipocket's retailers. I unchecked the box for Amazon.com so that there would not be a conflict with the eBook uploaded to Amazon's DTP.

If, because I have a Mobipocket publisher account, the book would be distributed through Amazon.com, why would I publish instead through DTP? It's a matter of placement within Amazon's categories. Mobipocket only allows one category choice; DTP allows up to five categories in which my book can be listed.

With *Teen Mom* published for the Kindle and available on Amazon.com and through the Mobipocket eBookstore, I can provide links on my websites to help generate sales. To cover all bases, I will also publish it as a "glassbook" through Lightning Source. The glassbook is published in PDF format.

Curiously, when I searched Amazon's Kindle Store a few days later, the listing for *Teen Mom* was correct. However, when I searched "Books," a second Kindle version was listed with the notation "This title is not available for customers from: United States." The other version, the one that *is* available to all customers, was not listed in this particular search.

Clicking on my name in the Amazon.com listing brings up most of my books including the two Kindle versions of *Teen Mom* and the paperback book. There is no link to the Kindle version on either the paperback or hardcover versions. The hardcover book, published through Lightning Source, does not show up in searches, but it is listed as an available format in the paperback listing.

Recommended Reading: *Publish Your Book on the Amazon Kindle: A Practical Guide*, by Michael R. Hicks.

Distribution
& Marketing

Just having a book for sale on Amazon.com won't make the royalties pour in. It doesn't happen that way. Book sales require a lot of marketing effort to get the book in front of potential buyers. There are several million books listed on Amazon.com which means one a book will get lost in the mass of books unless something happens to make it stand out from the crowd.

All expenses incurred to write, print, store, market, sell, and distribute your book should be factored into the retail price. Your royalties from book sales probably will not cover your expenses to produce and market your book simply because most books don't sell huge numbers of copies. Sales are generated by marketing and marketing is something many authors either are not good at doing or feel is a chore beneath them.

I'm not going to go into detail about book marketing because there are far too many good books dealing specifically with that topic already. One book I highly recommend is Steve Weber's *Plug Your Book! Online Book Marketing for Authors*, published in 2007.

Distribution: Then

After self-publishing *Advice for an Imperfect Single World,* and getting what could have been a very expensive lesson about *printing* books, I took on book distribution. This was another area about which I knew very little although I'd dabbled in distribution more than 20 years earlier when I self-published a 36-page magazine-size book of dog racing strategies.

With 1,000 printed copies to sell, I sent sample copies to various racetracks and gambling bookstores. This produced a small distribution network which I was able to handle but many of the people I contacted would only accept the publication if it came through a wholesaler distributor.

Getting a wholesale distributor to handle my publication was hard work because no distributor wants to spend time and effort on a publication they don't think retailers will carry or that doesn't fit their distribution demographic. After several turndowns, my book was accepted by a major magazine distribution company. However, even with this expanded distribution, I didn't sell huge numbers of books.

This early experience provided good lessons in printing, warehousing, fulfillment, invoicing, and working with wholesale distributors. I learned about returns, lost, damaged or destroyed books, and not to count a book sold until a check is in hand.

Distribution: Now

Sometimes a little knowledge can be a hinderance and so it was when I decided to self-publish *Advice for an Imperfect Single World*. Although I had several "how to" books in my bookcase, they didn't cover distribution. Because I had to set up distribution for my earlier gaming book, I assumed it was my responsibility to set it up for *Advice*, also.

If I had originally published through CreateSpace, distribution, at least through Amazon.com, would have been clear cut. As it was, I took a convoluted publishing path beginning with CafePress, then Lightning Source, and eventually CreateSpace.

When I submitted *Advice for an Imperfect Single World* to Lightning Source for their POD services, I also signed up for Ingram's distribution service. I thought this would immediately get my book listed on Amazon.com but when it didn't appear as soon as I thought it should, I placed an order for fifty books and applied for an Amazon Advantage account.

Once the Advantage account was activated, I listed *Advice for an Imperfect Single World* in my inventory and waited for the book orders to come in. If the book had been a best-seller, this would have been an extremely costly mistake.

Through Amazon Advantage, I was the wholesale distributor for my book, just as I had been for my earlier gaming book. Occasionally, when Amazon sold a copy of the book, they would place an order for one or two copies for their warehouse. For each book sent to Amazon, I was paid retail minus 55% *when the book sold*. At a retail of $16.95 minus $9.32 (55% discount) minus $5.94 (printing cost) minus shipping *from* Lightning Source *to* me plus shipping *from* me *to* Amazon, I was losing more than $1 every time Amazon sold a book! Once I realized that I was duplicating distribution efforts, and losing money, I zeroed out the Amazon Advantage stock so Amazon would order books directly from Ingram.

When I received Amazon's email that POD publishers had to use Amazon's BookSurge or CreateSpace POD services if they wanted their paperback books listed for sale on Amazon.com, I set up a CreateSpace account and submitted the same *Advice* PDF files I had originally prepared for Lightning Source. This edict raised such an uproar among POD publishers that Amazon has apparently backed down on their requirement but having to use CreateSpace opened a new publishing/print source which I would not have considered otherwise.

Amazon offers three different programs: Affiliate, Marketplace, and Advantage. I belong to all three, selling books I own on Amazon.com through my Marketplace account, and linking to books on Amazon from my websites using Affiliate links.The Advantage account currently is out of stock. It's important to read the details of each program as well as the fine print.

Necessary Marketing Materials

I will only mention a few of the basic marketing materials that I believe any author should have. Do buy a copy of Steve Weber's *Plug Your Book! Online Book Marketing for Authors*, to get ideas for creating a complete marketing plan for your book(s).

Do have a website; it does not have to be complex in design or costly to maintain. Websites can start out small and grow over time. Some authors use the blog format to post fresh content, book excerpts, and keep readers advised of their current projects and their updated media appearances.

A link on every page of the site to your book on Amazon.com or in your CreateSpace E-Store is essential. I generally link to my books on Amazon.com even though I get less royalty for each book sold. Or, cut out the middlemen and sell your book directly to make even more profit. Regardless of how you do it, you must not only market your book on your website but also provide a way to purchase it.

Don't use a free hosting service. For less than $100 a year you can get your own domain name and web hosting account. You'll look much more professional with your own domain and site plus you'll be able to control what's on the site. Many companies offering free sites make their money by placing affiliate ads on the sites which draw site visitors away and generate income for the hosting company.

Domain names through GoDaddy.com are currently less than $11 a year (always get a .com domain), and hosting is less than $100 a year through RochenHost.com, LinkSky.com, or FatCow.com. If you have little or no experience setting up a website, I recommend LinkSky.com or FatCow.com as they provide free website creators that are easy to use and come with a large selection of website templates. If you're more experienced, check out the hosting options at RochenHost.com.

Once you have your own hosted domain, be sure to set up a POP email account and use it. There is no reason to market someone else when you should be marketing yourself. For example, you@yourdomain.com looks much more professional than you@hotmail.com.

If you purchase marketing materials through CreateSpace, the designs and information included will be limited by the templates they use. You can print marketing materials much cheaper through other online printing services, and have more freedom as to what is included, as long as you can produce the proper artwork. I use VistaPrint.com for business cards and postcards, and PrintPlace.com for bookmarks.

I think it's important for authors to have business cards. You'll want to give them to local bookstore owners and other distribution sources as well as include them with review copies of your book.

Bookmarks are an exceptional marketing tool. Between the front and back of the bookmark, there is usually enough room for a miniature of the cover, where to buy info, website and email address, and perhaps a short excerpt or review. Ask if you can leave quantities of your bookmarks at bookstores and other public and retail locations in your area.

Epilogue

This book took longer to write than I expected. Once I began the step-by-step process, I tried to keep the information simple but complete. I hope I have accomplished that. If there are sections that need further explanation, information that I have overlooked, or if what I have written has helped you to self-publish your book, please email the details to pat@halpi.com.

The section about CreateSpace was written twice. The first time I set this book up with CreateSpace, I planned to use their ISBN. That is what I suggest to first time authors so that they can quickly experience the thrill of actually having a printed book to hold.

As I began writing the section about Lightning Source, I revised the copyright and title pages so that they contained my ISBN and company information. At that point, it made little sense to keep working between two files, one for CreateSpace and the other for Lightning Source, when I could submit one file to both.

When I returned to CreateSpace to delete the original listing and set it up with my ISBN, changes had been made to the CreateSpace website that made the original text and images outdated. Even though change is inevitable, particularly in the fast-paced world of technology, I did not want to go to press with information that no longer applied *at press time*.

Deleting the first listing on CreateSpace also deleted the original cover file. Once I set up a new listing, I had the option of using Cover Creator to create a new cover or uploading the cover prepared for Lightning Source. I decided to work through the Cover Creator process to update that information and found a "glitch" that required a workaround.

When I designed the cover for my original CreateSpace listing, I projected a final page count of 160 pages. When I increased the page size and cut extraneous text, I ended up with 104 pages. (Note: actual page count is now 112.)

Lightning Source will print spine text on books with as few as 80 pages so I was surprised when Cover Creator required a minimum of 134 pages to include spine text. I put in a false page count in order to use Cover Creator but when I was ready to submit files, I deleted the Cover Creator cover and uploaded a cover file prepared using a CreateSpace cover template – which did have space for spine text.

I occasionally publish books with different cover designs so the cover submitted to CreateSpace is not the same cover I submitted to Lightning Source. When the same book is printed through different printers, which usually means different distribution, the cover enables me to see which one retailers are marketing which also tells me distribution source.

I hadn't planned on adding a section on ePublishing but it's difficult to ignore one of the fastest growing book markets in the world. With the aggressive marketing of the Kindle and Kindle books, and the number of digital books available, I felt it was necessary. It also gave me the push to turn *Teen Mom* into a Kindle book, a project that had been way down on my "to do" list.

Once this book was completed, I submitted it to CreateSpace for the preview copy. The cover file was approved without problem. There were errors in the dpi of images in the interior file, with dpi ranging from 99 to 150 on many of the graphics even though they were all 300 dpi when I saved them. Once I replaced all graphics in .png format with those in .tif format, the resolution was retained when the file was converted to PDF, and I resubmitted the interior file to CreateSpace.

Once the proof through CreateSpace looked good, I submitted the same interior file, and a different cover file, to Lightning Source.

If I do ePublish this book it will probably be as a Lightning Source glassbook. Glassbooks are encrypted PDF files; they keep the same page layout as the printed book. There is additional work involved to publish a glassbook because all cover art and interior graphics must be reduced to screen resolution to keep the glassbook from being unreasonably large.

Resources

The following following information is just a fraction of the resources available about and for authors and publishers. I have not listed the numerous regional associations for authors or publishers nor have I attempted to provide a complete list of all websites that could be useful. Being listed as a resource does not constitute an endorsement of the service, product, or association.

Books

Aiming at Amazon: The NEW Business of Self Publishing, by Aaron Shepard, Shepard Publications.

Beginnings, Middles & Ends, by Nancy Kress, Writer's Digest Books.

Book Design and Production: A Guide for Authors and Publishers, by Pete Mastrson, Aeonix Publishing Group.

The Complete Guide to Book Publicity, by Jodee Blanco, Allworth Press.

The Complete Guide to Internet Publicity: Creating and Launching Successful Online Campaigns, by Steve O'Keefe, Wiley Computer Publishing.

The Complete Guide to Self-Publishing: Everything you need to know to write, publish, promote and sell your own book, by Tom and Marilyn Ross, Writer's Digest Books.

Design Basics, by David A. Lauer and Stephen Pentak, Harcourt Brace.

The Desktop Publisher's Legal Handbook: A Comprehensive Guide to Computer Publishing Law, by Daniel Sitarz, Nova Publishing Company.

Digital Type Design Guide: The Page Designer's Guide To Working With Type, by Sean Cavanaugh, Hayden Books.

The Fine Print of Self-Publishing: The Contracts & Services of 45 Self-Publishing Companies – Analyzed, Ranked & Exposed, by Mark Levine, Bascom Hill Publishing Group.

The First Five Pages: A Writer's Guide to Staying Out of the Rejection Pile, by Noah Lukeman, Fireside.

The Frugal Editor: Put your best book forward to avoid humiliation and ensure success, by Carolyn Howard-Johnson, Red Engine Press.

How to Publish and Promote Online, by M.J. Rose and Angela Adair-Hoy, St. Martin's Griffin.

How to Publish, Promote, and Sell Your Own Book: The Insider's Guide to Everything You Need to Know About Self-Publishing, From Pasteup to Publicity, by Robert Lawrence Holt, St. Martin's Press.

How To Start & Run a Small Book Publishing Company: A Small Business Guide To Self-Publishing And Independent Publishing, by Peter I. Hupalo, HCM Publishing.

How to Write Tales of Horror, Fantasy & Science Fiction, edited by J.N. Williamson, Writer's Digest Books.

Immediate Fiction: A Complete Writing Course, by Jerry Cleaver, St. Martin's Griffin.

The Joy of Writing Sex: A Guide for Fiction Writers, by Elizabeth Benedict, Holt Paperbacks.

Kirsch's Handbook of Publishing Law: For Authors, Publishers, Editors, and Agents, by Jonathan Kirsch, Silman-James Press.

Non-Designer's Design & Type Books: Design and Typographic Principles for the Visual Novice, by Robin Williams, Peachpit Press.

Perfect Pages, by Aaron Shepard, Shepard Publications.

Plug Your Book! Online Book Marketing for Authors, by Steve Weber, Weber Books.

The Self-Publishing Manual Volume II: How to Write, Print and Sell Your Own Book Employing the Latest Technologies and the Newest Techniques, by Dan Poynter, Para Publishing.

Start Your Own Self-Publishing Business: Your Step-by-Step Guide to Success, by Jennifer Dorsey and Entrepreneur Press.

Telling Lies for Fun & Profit: A Manual for Fiction Writers, by Lawrence Block, Harper Paperbacks.

Writing the Memoir: From Truth to Art, by Judith Barrington, The Eighth Mountain Press.

Writing With a Purpose, by James A. McCrimmon, Houghton Mifflin Company.

ePublishing Information

Amazon Digital Text Platform: http://dtp.amazon.com

Mobipocket: http://www.mobipocket.com

Flip At Once: http://www.flipatonce.com

SmashWords: http://www.smashwords.com

Graphics & Freelancers

ClipArt.com: http://www.clipart.com

Guru: http://www.guru.com

Self-Publisher Services

BowkerLink: http://www.bowkerlink.com

Library of Congress: http://www.loc.gov

Lightning Source: http://www.lightningsource.com

U.S. Copyright Office: http://www.copyright.gov

U.S. ISBN Agency: http://www.isbn.org

Publishing Discussion Groups & Forums

http://groups.yahoo.com/group/ebook-community

http://finance.groups.yahoo.com/group/pod_publishers

http://groups.yahoo.com/group/publishingdesign

http://finance.groups.yahoo.com/group/self-publishing

http://www.pub-forum.net

http://www.publaw.com

http://www.publishersweekly.com

http://www.publishersmarketplace.com/lunch/free

http://www.publish-l.com

Associations

American Society of Journalists and Authors: http://www.asja.org

Association of American Publishers: http://www.publishers.org

Audio Publishers Association: http://audiopub.org

Authors Guild: http://www.authorsguild.org

Authors & Publishers Association: http://www.authorsandpublishers.org

Children's Book Council: http://www.cbcbooks.org

Christian Small Publishers Association: http://www.christianpublishers.net

Educational Book and Media Association: http://www.edupaperback.org

Independent Book Publishers Association: http://www.ibpa-online.org

New York Center for Independent Publishing: http://nycip.org

PubNet: http://www.pubnet.org

Small Publishers, Artists, and Writers Network: http://www.spawn.org

Small Publishers Association of North America: http://spannet.org

Subsidy Publishers

BookLocker: http://www.booklocker.com

BookSurge: http://www.booksurge.com

CreateSpace: http://www.createspace.com

Harlequin Horizons: http://www.harlequinhorizons.com

Infinity Publishing: http://www.infinitypublishing.com

Lulu: http://www.lulu.com

Outskirts Press: http://www.outskirtspress.com

Xulon Press: http://www.xulonpress.com

About the Author

PAT GAUDETTE is an author, publisher, and website developer. She is the author of *How to Survive Your Husband's Midlife Crisis: Strategies and Stories From the Midlife Wives Club*, *Advice for an Imperfect Single World*, *Advice for an Imperfect Married World*, *Midnight Confessions: True Stories of Adultery*, *Teen Mom: A Journal*, and *Sparky the AIBO: Robot Dogs & Other Robotic Pets*.

She is the founder of popular relationship-oriented websites including *The Midlife Club* (MidlifeClub.com) and the award-winning *Friends and Lovers the Relationships Guide* (FriendsandLovers.com). She and her husband, Gerry, live in Florida.

Email her at: pat@halpi.com

Visit her website: www.patg.com

**How to Survive Your Husband's Midlife Crisis:
Strategies and Stories from The Midlife Wives Club**

Authors: Pat Gaudette & Gay Courter
Paperback: 288 pages
Publisher: Perigee Trade. (May 6, 2003)
ISBN-10: 0399528822
ISBN-13: 978-0399528828

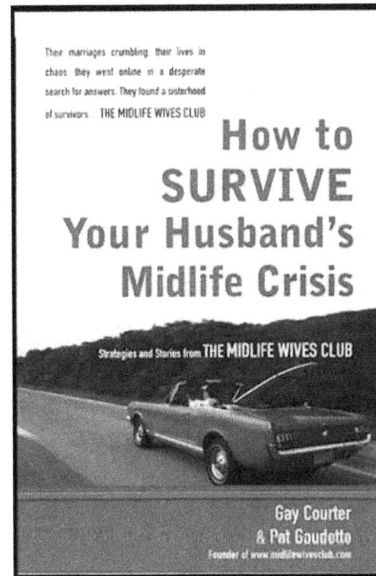

You've heard all the jokes about men's midlife crises – the new sports car, the new exercise regimen... and the new girlfriend. But when you're the wife trying to cope, it's no laughing matter.

A midlife crisis can devour a relationship. It may be devouring yours. The Midlife Wives Club is a supportive sisterhood for midlife mates – a chance to vent some steam, share advice, or just get a reminder that you're not alone. In this guide, you'll find wisdom from both midlife wives and experts on:

- *Recognizing* the symptoms
- *Coping* with the threat (or reality) of infidelity
- *Identifying* underlying problems like depression and anger
- *Deciding* when to stick it out – and when to pack it in
- *Protecting* your kids from the fallout
- *Making it through the crisis*... and coming out stronger, saner, and more self-reliant

With personal stories from real women (and men) and a comprehensive list of resources, **How to Survive Your Husband's Midlife Crisis** can help you get past the rough spots – and turn this tumultuous time into a change for the better.

Available in bookstores and online through Amazon.com and other retailers.

For immediate support for midlife issues visit www.MidlifeClub.com.

Teen Mom: A Journal

Edited by: Pat Gaudette
Paperback: 286 pages
Home & Leisure Publishing, Inc. (Nov 3, 2008)
ISBN-10: 0976121085
ISBN-13: 978-0976121084
Kindle & eBook Editions also available

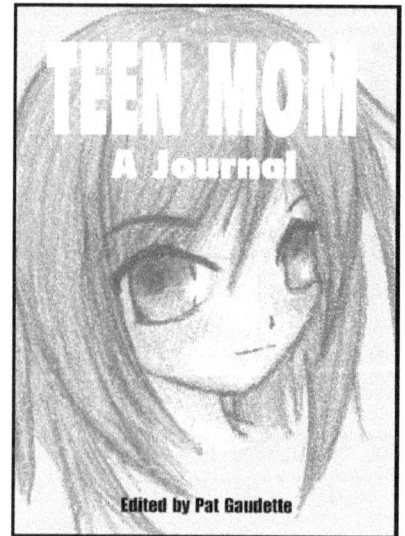

Sixteen-year-old "Katie" was half way through her junior year of high school when she became pregnant. Throughout her pregnancy and for several months afterward, she kept a journal. This is her story as told in that journal.

Katie is not one teenager dealing with unplanned pregnancy, she is one of many. She may be the girl next door or the girl in the next block. She may be your daughter. She may be *you.*

Teens are more openly sexually active than in past generations and unplanned pregnancy is not the social stigma of years ago. The pregnancy of pop idol Britney Spears' 16-year-old sister, actress Jamie Lynn Spears, was good fodder for the media but it didn't cause her to lose a starring role in *Zoey 101*, a television show drawing a large viewership aged 9-14. When vice-presidential candidate Sarah Palin announced her 17-year-old daughter, Bristol, was five months pregnant, it gave teen pregnancy even more of a stamp of "normalcy."

What is it like to be a pregnant teen? Let teen mom Katie tell you about it. She is one of more than half a million teens facing unplanned pregnancies each year according to data from *The National Campaign to Prevent Teen and Unplanned Pregnancy.*

Available in bookstores and online through Amazon.com and other retailers.

Midnight Confessions: True Stories of Adultery

Author: Pat Gaudette

Paperback: 251 pages

Home & Leisure Publishing, Inc. (Jan 1, 2005)

ISBN-10: 0976121042

ISBN-13: 978-0976121046

Kindle & eBook Editions also available

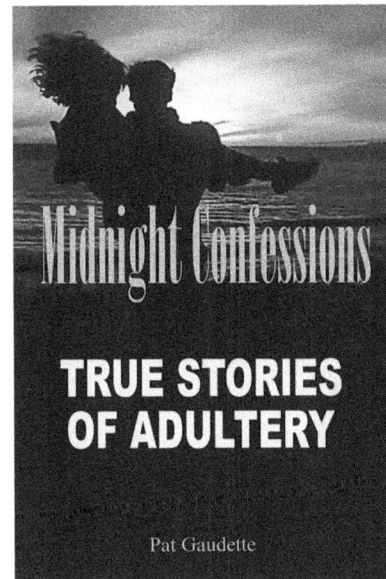

Why does a person cheat? What type of person cheats? What type of person loves a cheat? Can adultery be forgiven? Can a marriage survive the adultery of one or both partners? Can a cheater be trusted not to cheat again?

Love and lust are powerful forces but with enough time and tears each of us comes to a point of decision making when faced with betrayal.

If you are the betrayed spouse, do you confront? Do you leave? Do you get revenge by cheating? If you are the betrayer, do you lie or tell the truth? Do you keep the affair going or end it to save your marriage? If you are the other person, do you accept what you can get or do you force confrontation to "get it all"?

Midnight Confessions: True Stories of Adultery examines adultery from the adulterer's point of view, as well as that of the betrayed spouse and the other person. These are their stories in their words. Perhaps after reading their stories and the thought-provoking discussions in this book you will have a better understanding of the decision you need to make to fit your situation.

Available in bookstores and online through Amazon.com and other retailers.

Sparky the AIBO: Robot Dogs & Other Robotic Pets

Author: Pat Gaudette

148 pages
Home & Leisure Publishing, Inc.
ISBN 978-09761210-7-7 Paperback
ISBN 978-09761210-6-0 Hardcover

On January 26, 2006, Sony Corporation announced they were discontinuing development and production of their AIBO Entertainment Robots. Sparky the AIBO takes a look at this wonderful consumer robot beginning with the ERS-110, released in 1999, through the exceptionally complex ERS-7M3, released October 2005.

Models, software, accessories, forums, and web resources make this a must-have book for the AIBO enthusiast or the person interested in learning more about this delightful robot pet.

Amazon.com Customer Review:

"Very nicely written and a cute book. It goes into each models of Aibo and their history. And, the writer's personal experiences with her Aibos. If you ever wonder why Aibo owners love their Aibo, read this book."

Available in bookstores and online through Amazon.com and other retailers.

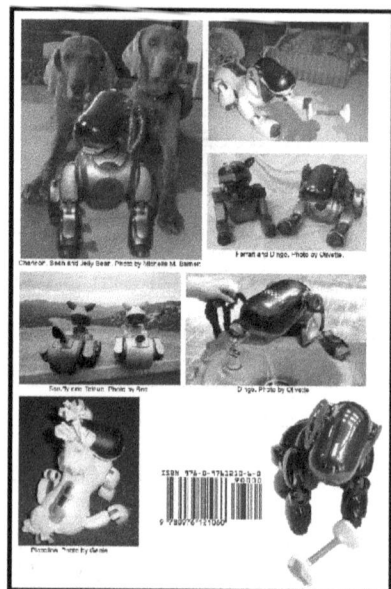

Advice for an Imperfect Single World

Author: Pat Gaudette
Paperback: 336 pages
Home & Leisure Publishing, Inc. (Sept. 9, 2004)
ISBN-10: 097612100X
ISBN-13: 978-0976121008
Kindle & eBook Editions also available

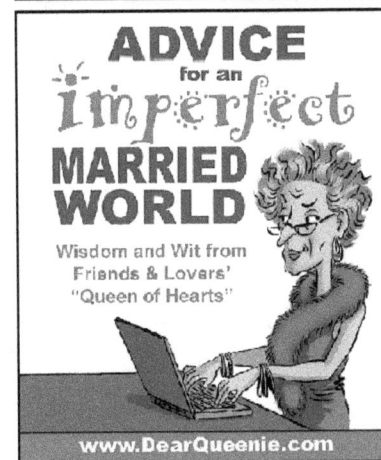

Advice for an Imperfect Married World

Author: Pat Gaudette
Paperback: 283 pages
Home & Leisure Publishing, Inc. (Sept. 9, 2004)
ISBN-10: 0976121026
ISBN-13: 978-0976121022
Kindle & eBook Editions also available

The outspoken "Queen of Hearts" is rarely without an opinion and since 1996 she has been sharing her thoughts about relationships in her advice columnist for the *Friends and Lovers* Web site. In *Advice for an Imperfect Married World,* the feisty Queenie gives her no-nonsense opinions about situations facing married couples and couples involved in long term relationships. A companion book, *Advice for an Imperfect Single World,* focuses on dating issues.

"Dear Queenie, me and my wife have split up and now we're trying to get back but she wants to be friends and take it slow. I'm afraid that we will just be friends and that's all. I want to know if we can be good friends and still be husband and wife and how can I show her that I want both?" - Peter.

"Peter, what you're really asking is how do you fast forward through all the friendship stuff and get right down to having sex again. While sex may be your top priority, developing a strong friendship is hers. If you are serious about wanting to repair your marriage you'll put your sex drive on hold and work on the friendship for now." - Queenie